About the author

Eugenie Houston is an entrepreneurial businessperson backed by broad senior level Human Resource experience. She has held Human Resource roles at Morgan Stanley, UPS and at Esat Telecom Plc as HR Director. She has extensive business development and marketing experience.

Her books include

Working and Living in Ireland
(now in its 6th edition, over 30,000 copies sold)
Working and Living in America

Go Contracting in Ireland
Go Contracting in the UK

Smart Moves at Work in the UK

Nursing in America
(used extensively by healthcare employers throughout the USA)

Special editions (with your company's branding), site licence editions, sponsorship and advertising opportunities exist for all of these titles on an ongoing basis. For more information, see www.workingandliving.com or www.smartmovesatwork.com

Eugenie Houston accepts **interim Human Resource assignments**, ideally with a strong financial and/or business development focus - the more challenging the better! She can be contacted directly by email at ehouston@smartmovesatwork.com

Thanks!

to my parents

entrepreneurial types by whom the words

'job for life'

were never mentioned

Smart Moves at Work is dedicated

to **Maureen** and in memory of **Des**

Smart Moves

at

Work

in Ireland

Eugenie Houston

www.workingandliving.com
www.smartmovesatwork.com

Working and Living Publications
http://www.workingandliving.com

© 2004, 2005 Eugenie Houston

A catalogue record of this book is
available from the British Library

ISBN 1-904682-19-7

Cover design by amoebacreatives.com

Although the author and publisher have taken every care to
ensure that the information published in this book is correct at the
time of going to press, neither can take any responsibility for any
loss or damage caused to any person or entity as a result of acting
on, or refraining from acting on, any information published
herein. Professional advice should be obtained before entering
into any legally binding commitments.

CONTENTS

Smart Moves at Work - Contents

Smart Moves at Work - Contents

Help! You're being outsourced! p251

Exit p261

****

Smart Moves at Work - Contents

In each of my books I support the fundraising efforts of a children's charity. **Smart Moves at Work** supports the funding efforts of **Our Lady's Hospital for Sick Children** in Dublin. Children from all over Ireland travel here to be treated and, as you are aware, funds are needed to build a new hospital.

You'll find details on page 289.

Thank you <u>very much</u>!

****

I am interested in hearing about your workplace moves and experiences, smart and not-so-smart.

Please feel free to post your comments on my 'blog' at www.smartmovesatwork.com

Best of luck

Eugenie Houston

Don't let your work life just happen to you!

Caroline Stuttle was on a gap year when she was pushed to her death from a 30ft bridge in Bundaberg, Queensland, Australia on 10 April 2002. She had been travelling in Australia with a friend before starting a psychology course at Manchester University.

Caroline had been in Bundaberg only a few days, working as a tomato picker, when she was killed as she returned to a caravan park after making a phone call to her boyfriend in England. She fought to hold on to her handbag as a drug addict tried to wrestle it from her.

He then threw her over the 30ft bridge. Caroline died instantly of a fractured skull and severed spine as she hit the ground. Heartrending evidence in the trial of her murderer described how the *strap of her bag was found still clenched in her hands* when her remains were recovered.

Handing down the sentence, the Judge said: "Miss Stuttle should have been enjoying the holiday of a lifetime.... throwing her off a bridge in the dark in a strange country for a miserable few dollars killed her in the most dreadful way."

Her attacker has been convicted of murder and jailed for life. Justice has been done.

It's a horrible story isn't it?

We are all frequently reminded to hand over the money when confronted by a mugger. But what would you do? I know if my life was in danger my instinct would be to fight. What about you? What if your property was under threat? Would you react?

A *reaction* is made on *impulse*. You don't actually stop to think it out. You certainly don't have the time to reflect when you are facing a clear and present danger. You can take steps to protect your safety but you don't have complete control over what happens to you; you are under attack.

It's different in the workplace. You have a lot more control, believe or not. Non-physical workplace 'assaults' do happen. Irrespective of whether they excel at the work or not, people get bullied, fired, set up for phoney performance issues, are denied equal pay for equal work, are lied to and lied about, are the last to know their job is on the line. It happens.

Except that the warning signs are often there, we just don't always see them. So when disaster strikes, we react on impulse.

But there is another choice. Instead of being caught off-guard and having to react impulsively, you could *respond*. A response means weighing up the options so that you don't put your foot in your mouth, or act in a way that you later regret.

My point is that you don't have to let your work life simply happen to you

Think about it. With the benefit of hindsight, can you think of any situation that you now wish you had handled differently? Would you now take the other option if you faced those circumstances again?

A part of my work involves working with companies undergoing major change. That often means 'rationalisation', ie changes, redundancies, cost savings. If handled well, and with excellent communication, employees emerge from this process unscathed. If they lose their jobs, they receive a generous package and in many cases, walk straight into a new job, having participated in outplacement programmes. Generally, employees in such situations are well looked after. And they have the camaraderie of their colleagues to help ease the blow.

Through my work, I've noticed a considerable increase in people who are unhappy at work. Overworked and under-appreciated. Bullied. Discriminated against because of gender. Not paid the same as colleagues doing the same work. Not allowed to take full holiday entitlement. Not challenged. No opportunities for promotion. The list of complaints in endless.

Don't let your work life just happen to you!

These are individuals who do not have the benefit of well-planned communications, having their hands held by outplacement professionals, the prospect of a nice redundancy deal and the promise of a glowing reference. Actually, I shouldn't say 'they'. For 'they' do not have the empathy of their colleagues, or that feeling of 'we're all in this together'.

This is the person who for some reason is miserable at work. This person feels victimised and alone. He may be bullied, he may be set up for the sack, he may just be bored silly and fed up doing the same old job, day in, day out. His unhappiness may not even be work-related.

But what happens is that it gradually dawns on this individual that he is unfilled and unhappy at work. This discontent then magnifies as time passes, the person begins to obsess about the problem and, if he or she is not careful, can spend so much time in the depths of misery that his work suffers and then he really could face a justified performance complaint.

Meanwhile, the individual is focussed on one thought, which repeats itself endlessly in their minds: **"It's not fair!"**

Often, it takes a crisis to compel people to take action to improve their working life. *"What are my rights?"* is a frequent question from an unhappy employee, at this point often too worn out to deal effectively with the situation.

The purpose of ***Smart Moves at Work*** is to equip you with strategies to manage your career more smartly. While your rights are important, and you will find details of these throughout the book, the emphasis is not on getting public justice but on handling your workplace situations in a way that will make *you* happy.

From my experience as a HR Director, an owner-manager of my own business and from working closely with client companies undergoing major change, such as rationalisation following an acquisition, I often stress the importance of good communication. The responsibility for communication does not lie exclusively with the employer – it works both ways.

In *Smart Moves at Work*, I put it to you that even if you are not spoon-fed information, you can find out the information that will make a difference to the way you do your job and how you survive, thrive and prosper in the workplace. *Don't let your work life simply happen to you.*

The greater your knowledge and understanding of how businesses and organisations operate, from the product or service offered to the way financial decisions are made, the more you will be able to make smart moves at work.

Your employer runs the business like a business, so why not adopt the approach of running your career like a business too?

Irrespective of whether they operate in the private or voluntary sector, whether they are large or small, all organisations have activities in common:

- They need people
- They need funds to operate
- Those funds are generally gained through making sales
- Even a publicly funded organisation has to make a sales pitch to obtain funds
- They have in place budgets, sales plans, headcount plans
- Irrespective of need, decisions will be made on the resources available. Take a lot at our hospitals. Loads of cash in the health service somewhere, not enough nurses, so operations get cancelled
- In most cases, the prevailing resource will be financial. If there's no cash, you will not get a pay rise
- *Continuous growth* in incoming revenue is just as important as available funds. You may be a brilliant newspaper editor who has built up a product from scratch and has never presented a dodgy offering. If your employer is not pulling in sufficient advertising revenue,

they will ignore the maxim that 'we are all (only) as good as our last piece of work' and cursorily replace you with a 'name'. It hurts but it happens

- Well-run businesses make contingency plans. They ask 'what if?' By making career contingency plans, you can avoid being caught off-guard if something goes wrong in your career. You will find many strategies for dealing with tough workplace situations in this book. Familiarise yourself with them and consider how you would handle the situations described. That way, if the going gets rough at work, it will not be the first time you have given these matters any thought and you will have a plan in mind. It doesn't need to be at the forefront of your mind every day - let's not be paranoid – but some advance preparation will definitely pay off. Think of it as a form of training

- Well-run businesses will have an exit plan. It may mean a sale but not always. It simply may be good succession planning so that an entrepreneur can hand on his or her business. In career planning terms, you should plan where you want to be next year, in 2, 5 and 10 years' time.

Smart Moves at Work is based on the principle that instead of letting events happen to you in the workplace, you can control a lot of what happens to you. You will help yourself succeed at this by thinking of your career as a business – your business. You'll need strategies and skills in the following areas to achieve this.

Sales
It is essential to understand how to sell, even if this means grasping only basic sales techniques. All of us in some way **sell** in our work. Think about this. Do you have reason to influence anyone? Do you ever have to ask for a favour? ALL of these situations are examples of making a sale. Learn even basic sales

techniques, and apply them, and you will find it easier to influence others at work.

Finance

The finance function yields considerable control in an organisation. Understand the key elements that finance people consider and you will have a better chance of understanding the reasons behind their decisions. What's more, irrespective of what you are trying to persuade your organisation to do, the best approach is usually to translate it into numbers. Cost savings, increased revenue.

So, learn to speak and present your case in terms the finance decision-maker will understand. This way you are more likely to succeed, or indeed to reject an idea because the company has no money and move on. Very importantly, if you are in a job that has impact on your employer's revenues, keeping an eye on the company's financials will help you determine whether your job is safe or not. The warning signs are always there, if you know where to look.

Good communication

Are you clear in what you communicate? You'll find strategies in **Smart Moves** for communicating change and bad news, managing anger, deflecting panic attacks and making sales presentations.

Marketing and building your brand

All good businesses have a clear brand. This identifies what they do and what they stand for. Good marketing is also about keeping the competition at bay. In the workplace, your 'competition' may be a colleague angling for the same promotional opportunity, or it may be a bully. *Moving on, Moving Up* offers strategies for handling promotion, while *Meet the Bullies* outlines what you can expect from workplace bullies and how you can counteract the effects of their behaviour. Bullies win all the short-term battles, but it is possible to outsmart them. The most important strategy for dealing with bullies is to prevent them from hurting you. That takes practice. It does not mean enduring suffering with a stiff-upper lip (that kind of stress is not going to get you to a happy ripe old age). No, I'm talking about learning to regard bullying objectively, asking yourself if you accept or are affected by this behaviour, and being able to decide that you are not. Learn to let the bullying go right over your head.

Contingency plan
Things can go wrong unexpectedly in business, and in careers too. Bring prepared doesn't mean you are paranoid, simply that you're smart enough to leave yourself well-equipped to handle whatever obstacles get in the way of being content with your work life. This covers a range of eventualities: redundancy, receiving a **P45-o-gram** (ie getting fired unexpectedly), relocation, a poor pay review or a personal setback that means you are unable to work.

Crisis management
There are times when setbacks at work really do seem like the end of the world. You'll find strategies for coping with this now, and for learning how to minimise the effects negative stress has on you in the future. There will always be ups and downs at work, as elsewhere, but they don't always have to impose trauma on you. You can keep it in perspective.

Corporate social responsibility
This is something companies talk a lot about these days. Please encourage your employer to put its money where its mouth is by contributing to the fund to build a new National Children's Hospital. Perhaps you and your colleagues could also organise something to help? (page 289). **Thank you very much indeed!**

Exit strategy

You don't need to execute your exit strategy if you prefer to stay in your current job, however the reality is that frequently people find themselves faced with losing their job without any prior hint. Or is it that they didn't see the warning signs? It's a smart move to know where you'd like to be in 2, 5 and 10 years' time.

The very first step in your smart moves strategy should be learning how to defend against sudden attack. When a sudden attack is launched in the workplace, the initial reaction is often panic, distress, worry and regret. Even if you currently don't need to deploy these strategies, *now* is the time to learn them so that you'll have them tucked away if and when you do need to act quickly and in your own interests.

Show me the money!

It's all about cash

Your employer has tons of money, so why can't they give you a pay rise, extra holidays, a promotion? To understand how your employer makes decisions and how you can operate to achieve results that favour you, you need to understand how businesses (include non-profit organisations in this) operate.

A business needs cash to survive and prosper. It is the primary indicator of business health. While a business can survive for a short time without sales or profits, without cash it will die. For this reason the inflows and outflows of cash need careful monitoring and management.

Cash is the measure of an organisation's ability to pay its bills on a regular basis. This, in turn, depends on the timing and amounts of cash flowing into and out of the business each week and month - cash flow.

Business decisions are made for commercial reasons. Here are some of the many reasons why you should understand your employer's financials.

1.   All business decisions are fundamentally financial decisions
2.   If you want to get ahead in the workplace, you must have a good grasp of the importance of an organisation's financials. And you must present your plans in a format that's familiar to financial decision-makers. The bottom line is that if your proposal involves spending or bringing in money, the financial controller or director in going to have a say in it, either the power to veto or approve your proposal there and then, or because of their role in setting final budgets
3.   If there is no money to pay for it, your idea or request will not be implemented, no matter how brilliant it is

4.   You have a better chance of having your proposal accepted if you pitch it as a business benefit, not a complaint. Speak to financial and sales managers in a language they understand – their own.

5.   You may not be looking for a pay rise, but fighting to stay in a job. Even if it's not in your job description, ask yourself if there is anything you can do to financially benefit your employer, such as reducing spending on stationery, saving money by turning off the lights and heating in rooms that aren't in use, helping with credit control by chasing up on payments, introducing sales leads? You may be helping to protect your own job from redundancy.

Can't you tell how well your employer company is doing by what they appear to be spending?
It would be a mistake to judge the financial health and wealth of your employer purely by the material trappings it displays. The recent liquation announcement of *Compustore*, a large computer retail store, is a timely example. In early Autumn 2004, the company moved from one set of fine premises into flash new premises and promoted the move heavily on radio. A month or so later, the liquidation process started.

Very often the move to new premises is a sign that a business is doing well. Or is it? Is it really a sign of anything other than a change of address? Certainly, successful businesses do upgrade to bigger and better premises and good luck to them. Companies also move to new premises because their lease expires and they simply can't make the financial commitment to the new terms, including the inevitable rent increases. Moving premises is not an indication of financial stability or of financial difficulty. It's just a new address.

Nor is radio advertising a sign of the financial health of a business; it's simply a signal that the company is looking for more business. Immediately before *topjobs.ie* went bust, it embarked on an extensive, and expensive, advertising campaign across all kinds of media. A week or two later, they were gone. Advertising extensively tells you nothing about the financial stability or instability of a company. It is simply marketing.

What is the difference between cash and profit

So your employer seems to be doing very well. But are they making any money? Well, they may have a good turnover but still make a loss. Take a look at the financial pages and notice companies going into liquidation. Often, they have a high turnover (and end up owing the Revenue a fortune in unpaid taxes). But if your employer doesn't have the funds to service the business, then they risk overtrading.

Overtrading takes place when a business accepts orders, and tries to fulfil them at a level that cannot be supported by its working capital or net current assets. This means that it does not have enough cash and cannot obtain enough cash quickly. Overtrading is highly illegal.

So the point is, **don't confuse cash with profit**. Profit is the difference between the total amount your business earns and all of its costs, usually assessed over a year or other trading period. An organisation may be able to forecast a good profit for the year, yet still face times when it is severely strapped for cash.

Equally, a smaller business with lower turnover and a tight control over costs could be profitable.

To make a profit, most businesses have to produce and deliver goods or services to their customers before being paid. Unfortunately, no matter how profitable the contract, if a business does not have enough money to pay its staff and suppliers before receiving payment, it will be unable to deliver its side of the bargain or receive any profit.

To trade effectively and be able to grow, a business needs to build up **cash reserves** by ensuring that the timing of cash movements puts it in an overall positive cash flow situation.

Cash in and cash out

Put yourself in your employer's position. During the business cycle, you need more money flowing in than flowing out. This will allow you to build up cash reserves to plug cash flow gaps, seek expansion and reassure lenders and investors about the health of your business.

In reality income and expenditure cash flows rarely occur together; it's usually spend first, get paid later. Your aim must be to do all that you can to speed up the incoming cash and slow down the spending.

Cash inflows include
- Payment for goods or services from your customers
- Receipt of a bank loan
- Interest on savings and investments
- Shareholder investments

Cash outflows include
- Purchase of stock, raw materials or tools
- Wages, rents and daily operating expenses
- Purchase of fixed assets - PCs, machinery, office furniture, etc
- Loan repayments
- Dividend payments
- Income tax, corporation tax, VAT and other taxes

Many of your regular cash outflows, such as salaries, loan repayments and tax, have to be made on fixed dates. You must always be in a position to meet these payments, to avoid large fines and/ or a disgruntled workforce.

Show me the money!

To improve everyday cash flow you can:
- Ask your customers to pay sooner
- Use factoring (though widespread, if your company uses factoring habitually instead of occasionally, it is not a sign of a particularly healthy business)
- Ask for extended credit terms with suppliers
- Order less stock but more often
- Lease rather than buy equipment (or do without – do you really need it?)

You can also improve cash flow by increasing borrowing, or putting more money into the business. This is acceptable for coping with short-term downturns or to fund growth in line with your business plan, but shouldn't form the basis of your cash strategy.

The principles of cash flow forecasting
Cash flow forecasting enables you to predict peaks and troughs in your cash balance. It helps you to plan borrowing and tells you how much surplus cash you're likely to have at a given time. Many banks require forecasts before considering a loan.

Elements of a cash flow forecast
The cash flow forecast totals the sources and amounts of cash coming into your business and the destinations and amounts of cash going out over a given period. There are normally two columns: one listing forecast amounts and one listing actual amounts.

The forecast is usually done for a year or quarter in advance and divided into weeks or months. It is best to pick periods during which most of your fixed costs - such as salaries - go out. The forecast lists:

- Receipts

- Payments
- Excess of receipts over payments - with negative figures shown in brackets
- Opening bank balance
- Closing bank balance

It is important to base initial sales forecasts on realistic estimates. Otherwise an acceptable method is to combine sales revenues for the same period 12 months earlier with predicted economic growth. All forecast figures must relate to sums that are due to be collected and paid out, not invoices actually sent and received. The forecast is a live entity. It will need adjusting in line with long-term changes to actual performance or market trends.

Manage income and expenditure

Effective cash flow management is as critical to business survival as providing services or products. Below are some of the key methods to help reduce the time gap between expenditure and receipt of income.

Customer management

Define a credit policy that clearly sets out your standard payment terms. Issue invoices promptly and regularly chase outstanding payments. Use an aged debtor list to keep track of invoices that are overdue and monitor your performance in getting paid. Consider exercising your right to charge penalty interest for late payment.

Consider offering discounts for prompt payment

Negotiate deposits or staged payments for large contracts. It's in your customers' interests that you don't go out of business trying to meet their demands.

Show me the money!

Supplier management

Ask for extended credit terms. Incentives such as large or regular orders may help, but make sure you have a market to sell on to. Consider reducing stock levels and using just-in-time systems.

Buy major items at the end rather than the start of a VAT period. This can greatly improve your cash flow and may help plug a temporary cash flow gap.

Avoiding cash flow problems

No matter how effective your negotiations with customers and suppliers, poor business practices can put your cash flow at risk.

Look out for:

- Poor credit controls - failure to run credit checks on your customers is a high-risk strategy, especially if your debt collection is inefficient.
- Failure to fulfil your order - if you don't deliver on time or to specification you won't get paid! Implement systems to measure production efficiency and the quantity and quality of stock you hold and produce.
- Ineffective marketing - if your sales are stagnating or falling, revisit your marketing plan. Are you targeting your customers properly - or is one sales person bringing in all the business?
- Inefficient ordering service - make it easy for your customers to do business with you.
- Poor management accounting – keep an eye on key accounting ratios that will alert you to an impending cash flow crisis or prevent you from taking orders you can't handle. Ratio analysis is a good way to evaluate the financial results of a business in order to gauge its performance. Ratios can be more helpful than the use of raw statistics. They provide you with the means of comparing your business against different standards by

demonstrating the relationship between two figures on your business' balance sheet. This enables you to compare your own business for example, against industry standards. There are four main methods of ratio analysis - **liquidity, solvency, efficiency and profitability**. An example of an efficiency ratio is the calculation of stock turnover. **Stock turnover** is cost of sales divided by stock level. This ratio is divided into the days of the year indicating the average holding period. Speed of stock turnover varies by industry, but a lower stock turnover generally means lower profits.

- Inadequate supplier management - your suppliers may be overcharging, or taking too long to deliver.

What should you know about budgeting and business planning if you want to progress at work?

*Like many people in the workplace, you'd like to expand your responsibilities. You'd like to **manage**. There are two reasons why you should hone up on your financial skills. Firstly, getting a good handle on your organisation's financials will help you to equip yourself for career progression (an organisation's financials are critical to its success). Secondly, if you manage your career in the way you'd run a good business, you'll position yourself to review positive growth at the end of each year, instead of boring yourself and everyone else wondering why you're still stuck in the same rut as you were exactly a year ago. The truth can hurt, I know.*

I recently listened to a woman on Social Welfare describe on radio how she managed her very small funds through relentless planning and budgeting. The woman is on a CE scheme and planning to get a job. If she approaches her work in the way she runs her household finances she will be a real star for a lucky employer!

Creating a budgeting process is the most effective way to keep a business - and its finances - on track. If you aspire to moving up the career ladder and picking up more management responsibilities, then you need to understand, and to be able to implement, good business plans and budgets.

Perhaps you are running an entire business, or a division or department. Or maybe you're responsible for a much smaller cost or revenue unit (the company's stationery budget, the amount spent on taxis, the social club's budget, selling classifieds). It doesn't matter what role you currently fill; learn to make financial plans and budgets and you'll find it a great help in your quest to move upwards.

Annual performance planning

Once you've started in a new role it's easy to become immersed in day-to-day problem solving, dealing with issues and challenges as they arise. Resolve to devote time to creating and managing your budgets and regularly reviewing your business plan. This can help keep the money moving smoothly - allowing you to concentrate on growing the value that you add to the business.

The key benefit of annual business planning is that it gives you the opportunity to stand back and review your business performance and the factors affecting your career development. If you adopt a business planning approach to your own career, you are less likely to find yourself at the end of yet another year unhappy with the fact that you have no real results to show for your efforts. Although your manager and employer influence greatly what happens with your career, your job is not a life sentence and you can achieve results to help you advance within your current employment, or that you can use to get a better deal elsewhere. The ball is in your court. So, don't just talk about it, get on with it. *Just do it!*

Components of an your annual business/ career plan

The main aim of an annual career plan is to set out the strategy and action plan for your business (ie YOU). This should include a clear financial picture of where you stand - and where you expect to stand - over the coming year. Your annual business plan should include:

- An outline of changes that you want to make to your business (ie your career)

- Potential changes to your market, customers and competition – will you change employers, sector or speciality?
- Your objectives and goals for the year. Your goals should be **SMART** – specific, measurable, achievable (even at a push, go on aim high), realisable (if you're not an astronaut, a trip to space is not realistic) and time-specific (it's not 'I will one day' – state *when* and then achieve your goal by that date)
- Your key performance indicators
- Any issues or problems
- Any operational changes
- Your management and people. This includes your superiors, those who report to you and any influential colleagues or associates who may be in a position to help you out. This should include your network outside your current job – if you don't have any contacts, then it's time to start developing some
- Your financial performance and forecasts
- Investment in the business, ie in your skills set. Do you plan to gain new skills, obtain additional qualifications and build on your knowledge in some way? Some employers will help with the cost of this; equally, if you can, don't be afraid to invest your own time and money in enhancing your own skills. You will be more marketable as a result of additional and/ or updated qualifications.

Career planning using a business-planning model is most effective when it's an ongoing process. This allows you to act quickly where necessary, rather than simply reacting to events after they've happened. Here is a typical business-planning cycle, applied to your career:

- Review your current performance against last year/current year targets
- Work out your opportunities and threats, for instance are you aware of any upcoming developments that will mean new opportunities? Do you have the skills to fill any of these? Which new skills could you gain to position yourself better for a win? What's the competition like?
- Analyse your successes and failures during the previous year
- Set out your key objectives for the coming year
- Identify and refine the resource implications of your review and build a budget.
- If you are in a revenue-generating role, define the new financial year's profit-and-loss and balance sheet targets
- Review your plan regularly - for example, on a monthly basis - by monitoring performance, reviewing progress and achieving objectives.

Budgets and business planning

A **budget** is a plan to control your finances. It enables you to make confident financial decisions, meet your objectives and ensure you have enough money for your future projects. It outlines what you will spend your money on and how that spending will be financed. At the same time, it is not a forecast. A forecast is a *prediction* of the future whereas a budget is a *planned outcome* of the future, as defined by your plan, that you want your business (career) to achieve.

If you have any shred of responsibility for revenue or operating expenses in your job (this includes managing other people), then you should have a budget. You will better able to:

- Manage your money effectively
- Allocate appropriate resources to projects
- Monitor performance

Show me the money!

- Meet your objectives
- Improve decision-making
- Identify problems before they occur - such as the need to raise finance or cash flow difficulties
- Plan for the future
- Increase staff motivation

There are a number of key steps you should follow to make sure your budgets and plans are as realistic and useful as possible.

Allow time for budgeting. It's worth setting aside some time to fully consider all the elements of your budget. If you invest some time in creating a comprehensive and realistic budget, it will be easier to manage and ultimately more effective.

Use last year's figures - but only as a guide. Collect historical information on sales and costs if it is available. But it's essential also to consider what your sales plans are, how your sales resources will be used and any changes in the competitive environment.

Create realistic budgets **using the historic information**, your business plan and any changes in operations or priorities to budget for overheads and other fixed costs.

It's useful to work out the **relationship between variable costs and sales** and then use your sales forecast to project variable costs. For example, if your unit costs reduce by 10 per cent for each additional 20 per cent of sales, how much will your costs decrease if you have a 33 per cent rise in sales? If you are preparing a career budget, work out the relationship between your net pay and your outgoings. Do you need to earn more? How will you achieve that?

Make sure your budgets contain enough information for you to easily monitor the **key drivers** of your business such as sales, costs and working capital. In your career budget, the key drivers would be gross pay, tax deducted, net pay, benefits such as pension and health coverage, costs such as childcare and travel. If you drive to work and spend a couple of thousand euro every year on parking, the smart move may be to live closer to your job, or move jobs to be closer to your home. You might decide to avail of the advantageous tax treatment of renting out a room in your home or taking an employer-provided annual travel ticket and should factor items such as this into your budget.

Involve the right people. If any of your staff or colleagues have financial responsibilities - for example sales targets, production costs or specific projects - it's a good idea to get them involved at the planning stage so they understand the budget and feel comfortable working with it. Once they do, you can give them the responsibility for sticking to the budget. On your career budget, you may want to include the earnings and outgoings of your partner too.

Checklist: what your budget should cover

First you need to decide how many budgets you really need.
Many small businesses have one overall operating budget that sets out how much money is needed to run the business over the coming period - usually a year. As your business grows, your total operating budget is likely to be made up of several individual budgets such as your marketing budget, for example, or your sales budgets. A single budget will probably be fine for your career calculations, although a detailed breakdown of your business and personal outgoings should be included.

Your budgets will need to include the following, however they are allocated:

Projected cash flow - your cash budget projects your future cash position on a month-by-month basis. Budgeting in this way is vital for small businesses as it can pinpoint any difficulties you might be having. It should be reviewed at least monthly. Review your personal budget and outgoings regularly too; if you are contemplating making a career move that will impact your finances, you must have a realistic understanding of whether you can afford it.

Costs - typically, your business will have three kinds of costs:

> **Fixed costs:** eg rent, rates, salaries and financing costs
> **Variable costs**: including raw materials and overtime
> **One-off capital costs**: may include purchases of computer equipment or premises for example

Your **personal/ career budget** will have similar categories:

> **Fixed costs:** rent or mortgage, household bills, loan repayments
> **Variable costs:** medical expenses, holidays, and transport
> **One-off costs:** cost of further training/ education

To forecast your business costs you can either look at last year's records or contact your suppliers for quotes. For your personal budget, it is recommended to allow for something unforeseen – the equivalent of at least 3 months' pay tucked away for a rainy day is advisable. A tough stretch for many, I know, but worth it.

Revenues - sales or revenue forecasts are typically based on a combination of your sales history and how effective you expect your future efforts to be. In terms of personal earnings, it is best not to overemphasise overtime and bonus payments. Make an informed assumption by all means, but don't get carried away by your expectations.

Using your sales/ earnings and expenditure forecasts, you can prepare projected profits for the next 12 months. **This will enable you to analyse your margins and other key ratios such as your return on investment.** In career terms, if you have spent a considerable of time and money gaining a new qualification, then, provided you *apply* your new qualification, you should expect to see a return on this investment at some point.

Use your budget to measure performance

If you base your budget on your business/career plan, you will be creating a kind of financial action plan. This can serve several useful functions, particularly if you review your budgets regularly as part of your annual planning cycle.

Your budget can serve as:

- An indicator of the costs and revenues linked to each of your activities
- A way of providing information and supporting management decisions (including how you manage your career) throughout the year
- A means of monitoring and controlling your business (or career), particularly if you analyse the differences between your actual and budgeted income

Benchmarking performance

Benchmarking has become a bit of a dirty word (unless you're in the public sector, in which case congratulations!) but comparing your budget year-on-year can be an excellent way of benchmarking your business performance - you can compare your projected figures, for example, with previous years to measure your performance. Apply the same calculation to your compensation (salary, overtime and bonus payments, paid holidays, benefits). Are you better off financially this year compared to last? If not, identify the reason, determine what you need to do to change that situation going forward and then *do it*.

You can also compare your figures for projected margins and growth with those of other companies, or across different parts of your business. If you apply this principle to your personal career budget, compare your figures with those of peers in competitor companies; if you don't have this information, phone a couple of recruitment agencies and ask. You'll get a good indication of the rates on offer for positions they are currently handling. (Though I wouldn't put too much faith in the 'annual salary surveys' that some agencies produce. These serve well as a clever marketing tool, which is all they are intended to be. Compiling salary surveys is a fairly complex and specialised activity).

Key performance indicators

To boost your business' performance you need to understand and monitor the key "drivers" of your business - a driver is something that has a major impact on your business. There is a multitude of factors that affect the performance of every business, so it is vital to focus on a handful of these and monitor them carefully. For example:

key areas business	key areas career
Sales	Salary, benefits, bonus, holidays
Costs	Mortgage, rent, travel, childcare, work clothes, parking, domestic bills, loans, credit card repayments
Working capital	Net pay after all of your essential costs are paid (you may decide to forego a car, but items such as housing are not discretionary)

Any trends towards cash flow problems or falling profitability will show up in these figures measured against your budgets and forecasts. They can help you spot problems early on if they are calculated on a consistent basis.

To use your budgets effectively, you will need to frequently review and revise them. This is particularly true if your business is growing and you are planning to move into new areas. Using up-to-date budgets enables you to be flexible and to manage your cash flow and identify what needs to be achieved in the next budgeting period.

Two main areas to consider
First, your actual income - each month compare your **actual income** with your sales budget, by:

- Analysing the reasons for any shortfall - for example in business that could be lower sales volumes, flat markets, under performing products. In career and personal financial terms, it could be lower overtime payments, expected bonus didn't materialise, your tenant left
- Analysing the reasons for a particularly high turnover - for example whether your targets were too low

Compare the timing of your income with your projections and check that they fit.

Analysing these variations will help you to set future budgets and also allow you to take action where needed.

Second, your **actual expenditure** - regularly review your actual expenditure against your budget. This will help you to predict future costs with better reliability. You should:

- Look at how your fixed costs differed from your budget
- Check that your variable costs were in line with your budget. Normally variable costs adjust in line with your sales volume
- Analyse any reasons for changes in the relationship

- Analyse any differences in the timing of your expenditure. For instance, you may have overlooked credit card repayments when compiling your personal budget.

Having completed this exercise, can you see the close alliance between managing your business and personal finances? Of course, there are differences in scale and complexity, but the basic principle remains the same. Take in as much cash as you can, conserve it and spend as little as possible.

You have been overpaid. Can you keep the money?

Your employer has mistakenly over-paid one of your expense claims by several thousand euro. You want to know whether you are legally obliged to return this money?

This is a serious situation. Put everything in writing in a clear, factual and unemotional manner.

You have a duty of good faith to your employer to return the overpayment as soon as possible.

What's more, it is not simply a question of whether or not to return the money. Keeping the money and failing to *disclose* that you received the overpayment is likely to constitute a breach of good faith.

Such a breach could amount to gross misconduct and lead to **summary dismissal**. A summary dismissal does not require the same level of fair procedure as a normal dismissal. The scale and severity of the misconduct justifies the immediate termination of the employment relationship. Where someone is dismissed summarily, there is no obligation on the employer to observe either the contractual or statutory notice periods. So you could be booted out with nothing, including no reference. Yes, even though the initial mistake was not yours.

You should also be aware that your employer is entitled to deduct the amount of the overpayment, as a single payment, if they wish, from your salary without obtaining written consent from you. You can, however, ask to pay by instalments.

If you are the employer in this situation, think before you act. Consider whether a disciplinary procedure is more appropriate; ask yourself whether the amount of time that has lapsed between the employee's knowledge of the overpayment and his failure to act on it was reasonable, ie long enough. Check that the employee does know the overpayment has been made.

If you are an employer looking for a way to get rid of an employee, forget about an 'accidental' overpayment as a contrived means to achieve your aim.

Orchestrated 'exits', either by an employer to fire an employee or by an employee looking for a payoff, will backfire, prove expensive and cannibalise reputations. Although you are not compelled to, consider paying the statutory and contractual notice periods anyway.

And take a close look at your financial controls!

Can you use a 'better offer' from a competitor to get more money in your current job?

If you receive an offer of a better package from a competitor, but don't really want to move jobs, what is the best way to capitalise on this with your current employer? Should you just tell your boss what you've been offered? What if he calls your bluff and doesn't offer to improve your package?

Wow, risky strategy and not a well calculated risk. I don't recommend this approach at all and I would urge you not to make employment decisions based solely on salary/package.

You're probably right to guess that rather than give you an increase in pay, your current employer might simply wish you good luck with your new job.

You say you don't really want to move jobs. What elements of your current role encourage you to stay? The work itself? Challenging role? Good colleagues? Your employers treat people fairly? Convenient location? Hours are fair? Pay is market rate? Benefits suit you? Prospects for advancement?

If you have an offer from a competitor, take it only if its better in more respects than your existing job. Will you be working with a great bunch of people who you can learn with? Will the move enhance your career prospects in the future? Is it a better "name" in your sector of the market?

If you can't answer yes to these kinds of questions, I'd advise you to be very wary of moving just for the money.

How can you measure the cost of hiring the wrong person?

lost people = lost profits

As the Celtic Tiger Mark 2 looms, have you noticed how many recruitment agencies are advertising for new staff? They are all gearing up for the massive recruitment explosion. They make a lot of money and will continue to do so.

Most HR professionals and their financial peers bemoan recruitment fees. But they are just part of the total financial damage inflicted by excessive employee turnover.

As a rule, each manager or professional who resigns costs the company the equivalent of 18 months' salary. Non-management workers cost about 6 months' pay. This cost includes money spent on direct replacement expenses such as advertising, recruiter's fees and employee development.

This does not include, however, indirect opportunity costs such as lost sales, lower productivity and customer defections. These latter costs are much harder to quantify and may be even more damaging to companies than the direct costs of employee turnover.

Imagine a company with 5,000 employees who earn an average of €23,000. Turnover rate of 14 per cent for administrative and operations employees, 12.5 per cent for professionals and sales staff ('professionals' don't earn overtime payments) and 5.5 per cent among managers could collectively cost more than €13 million annually.

For companies with annual revenues of €325 million, this loss would represent 4 per cent of total revenues. That's 40 per cent of profits, assuming the company earned 10 per cent on revenues

Smart Moves at Work

The costs of employee turnover are proportionately comparable for smaller and larger organisations. A company with 1,000 employees would incur annual employee turnover costs of €2.70 million; a company with 20,000 employees would lose €55.76 million.

Show me the money!

Calculating redundancy pay

Your company has made you redundant after two years and 10 months' employment. You are being offered a payment of two weeks for each full year of employment. Is it not common for companies to round up the years, in this case to three? Should your car allowance also be added to this figure?

The simple answer is that the company is not obliged to round up years in the absence of a contractual entitlement, whether express or as a result of any custom or practice to the contrary.

You are entitled to a statutory redundancy payment. For each complete year of service between the ages of 16 and 66, you are entitled to two week's pay, plus a bonus week. Statutory redundancy payments are tax-free.

A "week's pay" is capped €600 from 1 January 2005 (€507.90 prior to that). Your car allowance would be included for the purpose of calculating your week's pay under the statutory formula but subject to the cap. In the absence of any further contractual right your employer would not have to include the car allowance if you are receiving a payment based on actual (rather than capped) pay and this exceeds the €600 cap.

You will also need to check whether you have any contractual entitlement in addition to the statutory formula. Employers sometime agree to pay more than the statutory entitlement, or are prepared to remove the cap on the week's pay. In the absence of this, you will be entitled to the statutory minimum.

Finally, there is the question of whether you have been given formal notice to terminate your employment. Your statutory minimum notice would be two weeks but your contract may well entitle you to a longer period. If your employment has been terminated without notice you would be entitled to pay in lieu as well as your redundancy payment.

Can you claim for equal pay with male colleagues?

You have been working in your firm for over two years. You found out early on that a colleague of the same age and experience was paid 30% more than you. When you raised this you were told it was because his previous salary was quite high. After two years, the gap is widening, he has received a pay rise and you are still waiting to hear about yours. What are you entitled to do?

You may be able to launch a claim for equal pay under the Employment Equality Act.

In order to be successful in a claim for equal pay, you will need to show that you do work which is the same or broadly similar to the work done by your colleague. If you cannot show that, then you can still succeed if your work is of equal value to his, in terms of such factors as the demands made on you (for instance under headings such as effort, skill and decision-making responsibility).

If you can prove one of these comparisons and you are earning less than your colleague, then it is up to your employer to show that the reason for the difference in your salaries is a *material* factor, which is not the difference of gender.

Examples of material factors that can justify unequal pay are if your colleague has greater experience or extra qualifications that are relevant to the job. However, in this case it seems likely that your employer will try to rely on 'market forces'. In other words, your employer will say that the only way in which it could recruit and retain your colleague was by paying him a higher salary.

The question of when it is or is not acceptable for an employer to justify pay differentials by relying on market forces is not easy to answer. The answer to the question depends largely on the circumstances in each case.

As a general rule, relying on market forces is a legitimate defence. However, an employment tribunal will examine the argument in each individual case in order to ensure that there is no hidden sex discrimination in the reliance on market forces. So, for example, if the men in your organisation are being paid more, on average, than the women because of the use of market-related factors in setting their wages, then the employer will have to go one step further and show that it is necessary and proportionate for it to rely on the market as a way of setting wages.

To do this, it would need to provide evidence that it had to pay certain individuals more than others because, for example, they brought to the job skills which were in short supply and which were needed in the business.

The bottom line is that the market forces defence will not work if in reality it amounts to paying women less simply because they will work for less.

Can they cut your pay?

Your employer has told you that you are now in a consultation period because you are supposedly "overpaid" for doing a "similar" job to somebody else who is paid less. They want you to take a pay cut and possibly an increase in hours. The other person and you work together, have been with the company for five years, earning the same for two years. What are your rights?

The simple answer is that your employer cannot change any terms and conditions relating to your pay or your duties without your consent and you can refuse to agree to such changes.

Sometimes employees do consent to such changes where the only alternative is to be made redundant because, for example, the business will have to close without the changes.

You should clarify with your employer what they mean by a "consultation period", as this is normally used in the context of consulting before someone is dismissed by reason of redundancy. Being "overpaid" in your employer's eyes is certainly not the same thing as being made redundant. In particular, you should ask them what they intend to do if you refuse.

You also need to check your terms and conditions of employment relating to your duties, which again, your employer cannot change without your consent to increase your work burden.

The "duties" clause in any contract you may have is highly likely to be very broadly drafted and that is why it is important to check any such contract.

You should also ask your employer why they are not considering raising your colleague's salary rather than reducing yours. It may well be that your colleague is carrying out a similar job to yours and has complained that he or she is not being paid enough in comparison to you, in which case they should be given a salary increase rather than a reduction being imposed on you.

If your employers do attempt to reduce your salary without your consent you may have at least three claims.

The first claim is for "unlawful deduction of wages" and the claim is for any shortfall in the wages you are entitled to receive. You do not have to resign to make such a claim, but would need to bring a claim within six months of the sum being payable (or, if a series of deductions, within three months after the last deduction).

Second, you could also bring a claim for breach of contract in the civil courts, unless your employment ends in which case you can bring such a claim in an employment tribunal.

Third, the reduction in your salary alone would probably entitle you to resign and claim "constructive unfair dismissal", if you have one year's service or more. What this means is that you would have to resign promptly (ie if you delay and accept the reduced salary you could be deemed to have accepted changes in your terms and conditions). You should explain why you are resigning to your employer and assuming that this has caused you to resign, you would be able to bring a claim for unfair dismissal. **Don't ever resign in such circumstances without first urgently consulting a specialist employment solicitor.**

In addition to a straightforward claim for unfair dismissal and unlawful deduction of wages, you could also potentially have claims for discrimination if the reason for your employer treating you in the way that they have done is on any of the **9 grounds** set out in the Employment Equality Act. These are: gender; marital status; family status; age; disability; race; sexual orientation; religious belief and membership of the Traveller community. You do not have to resign to bring such a claim.

Recovering unpaid salary from an employer that has gone bust

The IT services firm you worked for recently went into liquidation, making all staff redundant. The administrators say there is no money for outstanding salaries or redundancy pay. The company's assets have been sold to another company with the same directors. Can you recover the money you are owed?

The law makes special provision in relation to wages owed to employees by insolvent employers. In this situation, an employee can apply to the Minster for Enterprise and Employment for payment of certain debts owed by the employer. These are:

- Normal weekly remuneration: up to a total of eight weeks' arrears, applying to a ceiling of €600 per week from 1 January 2005. This ceiling applies to all claims made to the fund, including sick pay, notice, etc

- Sick pay: any arrears up to 8 weeks' under a sick pay scheme that forms part of your contract of employment. Only the difference between disability or injury benefit and normal weekly remuneration is payable.

- Notice: amount payable under the Minimum Notice and Terms of Employments Acts as awarded by the Employment Appeals Tribunal

- Holiday pay: up to a maximum of 8 weeks

- Unfair Dismissals Acts: awards payable following a recommendation, determination, or orders from a Rights

Commissioner, Employment Appeals Tribunal or Circuit
Court

- Court awards for arrears of wages, sick pay and holiday
  pay are also covered

- Wrongful dismissal: a Court award for damages is also
  covered. However, the maximum amount will be limited
  to what would have been obtained as redress under the
  Unfair Dismissals Acts

- Employment Regulation Order: an amount payable under
  such an Order within the meaning of the Industrial
  Relations Acts, 1946 – 1990, where proceedings have
  been instituted

- Equal Pay or Equality – amounts payable following a
  determination, recommendation, or order under the Anti-
  Discrimination (Pay) Act, or the Employment Equality
  Act, further to Equality Officers', Labour Court of High
  Court award

- Unpaid employer contributions to pension schemes. This
  includes contributions from the employee which the
  employer has deducted from the employee's pay. The sum
  payable is the lesser of: balance of contributions
  remaining unpaid for 12 months on the day prior to
  insolvency or amount certified by an actuary to meet the
  liability of the scheme.

You say the company's assets have been sold to another company
with the same directors. This can now only happen if the
liquidator gives the 'all-clear' in terms of any wrongdoing in the
original company. Directors can no longer evade compliance.

Female colleagues earn more than you

You have become aware that female colleagues in your team doing the same job are being rewarded better than you because they were recruited externally. Although you would understand if the differentials related to knowledge and experience, it has become obvious that this is not the case. You are male. How can you raise this issue without it becoming a source of conflict?

This is a common but difficult situation. You are right that ultimately employers have to pay the market rate for external recruits, which is generally 10-15% above the going internal rate for the job.

So what can you do about it? You've said you don't want to cause conflict (I often hear this but sometimes a loud complaint does the trick). Anyway, you don't want to do that. Well, you have three choices.

Say and do nothing. It's what many people do. It would be an understandable choice, though it hardly qualifies as a smart move.

Discuss your pay with your manager in the context of your performance reviews – it doesn't matter if you are due a performance review or not. Act quickly, rather than accept the discrepancy any longer. Make the main argument that you think you're worth more because of the great job you are doing. Point out how much you enjoy the job. That's a constructive discussion. Then point out that, under the Employment Equality Act 1998, a person of one sex is entitled to be paid the same for the same work as a person of the other sex when both are paid by the same, or an associated employer.

If you think you can get a better paid job elsewhere, then find one and leave. Don't find a new and then try and blackmail a rise. This will not work and your employer will probably simply wish you good luck in your new job.

How can you make them pay promised redundancy?

You were made redundant after two years' service. The company wrote to you advising that they owed you for statutory redundancy, 3 month's notice, annual leave and car allowance. They have since paid you 20% of the amount owed, and say the rest depends on their obtaining further funding. What can you do?

It is helpful that your former employer has confirmed and accepts that it owes you a redundancy payment, money for your 3-month notice period, annual leave and car allowance as there can, at least, be no dispute as to liability, if you do have to take legal action to recover the balance of what is due to you.

Although your employers say they are waiting for funds in order to make such payments, do you know whether or not that is, in fact, true? If it is true, do you know when they anticipate having the necessary funds? The simplest course of action would be to write to your former employers if you have not already done so, asking them to pay the balance of the money owed to you within a specified timeframe or asking them to give you an alternative timeframe within which they anticipate being able to pay you this amount. Have you explored whether or not they would be able to pay any of it voluntarily in instalments?

If you think that they are not genuinely unable to pay you this amount, you could always warn that if they fail to make a payment by a particular date, you may be forced to issue proceedings against them for the recovery of these sums, or, if they are insolvent, formally seek a winding up order against them which would allow you to claim some of this amount from the Employer Insolvency Fund. You need to consider whether these types of threats are likely to assist you in seeking voluntary payment by them at this stage however.

If they fail to pay you these sums, you have two options.

Option 1

If your employer is technically insolvent (ie if a winding up or similar order has been made), you can apply to the Minster for Enterprise and Employment for the following payments to be made from Redundancy and Employer Insolvency Fund. These include:

(a) A redundancy payment

(b) A sum equal to pay in lieu of your statutory minimum notice period

(c) Up to 8 weeks' holiday pay

(d) Any arrears of pay (again subject to the €600 weekly cap from 1 January 2005) up to a maximum of 8 weeks

If no winding up order is in place, you could apply for one yourself. However, you would need to take advice on how to proceed on this basis and it may not be the most practical option if you think funds will be forthcoming.

Option 2

If you are not convinced that your employer is genuinely insolvent and unable to pay its debt to you, you could apply to the Employment Appeals Tribunal for an order that these sums be paid.

A tribunal claim against the company may pressurise them to focus on settling your outstanding debt more quickly than if you simply asked them to pay you voluntarily.

If you are going to bring a claim at an employment tribunal you should be aware that you have 6 months from the date of your dismissal within which to claim your statutory redundancy payment.

Show me the money!

As your employers have already accepted liability for these sums, the process should be fairly straightforward.

Unfortunately, if your employer genuinely does not have the funds to pay and this is the only reason they are not paying you, then a tribunal in itself would not be of much help to you. In this case, the Redundancy and Employers Insolvency Fund is your best bet. You will find details of forms and where to submit them on www.entemp.ie

How can you get your bonus?

Your employer of four years has just given you notice of termination due to major redundancies within the firm. You had a guaranteed bonus pay structure and feel aggrieved that although you have met this year's budget your (substantial) bonus will be lost and instead you get 3 months' base salary. Is there any way of taking them to a tribunal to get what you have worked so hard for during this past year?

The **purpose** of the bonus may be important - is it to provide an incentive to staff or is it a reward for past services? There is a lot of additional information that is required before being able to advise in detail. I do this deliberately here – since I am writing this, I could easily have added in as much detail as I want. But as well as answering this question on the information provided, I'd like to show the importance of seeking *advice specific* to all of the circumstances and details of your *own particular case*. Never assume that the remedy applied in someone else's case will *automatically* apply to yours.

Based on the detail provided in your question, it is possible that you may have a claim that you can bring before the Employment Appeals Tribunal and so you should arrange to see a solicitor or other legal adviser to discuss the specific circumstances of your case in detail.

Given that the bonus is part of your pay structure, it may well be expressed to be a contractual entitlement rather than a discretionary (and non-contractual) payment. You will need to look at the wording of any bonus documentation and your contract of employment.

However even if the bonus is contractual you may still not have a claim. You need to see what the conditions for payment are and what the timings are for payment. For example, the bonus may require you to be in the employment of the company at the time of payment. Therefore if the time of payment is after you have been made redundant, then the bonus will not be payable to you.

If the documentation is silent on these issues, then what the company has done with the bonuses in the past is very important. For example is there a custom of normally paying the bonus to employees even though they are no longer employed by the company? Even if the bonus is discretionary you may still have a valid claim.

Assuming that you have a claim for the bonus, there are a number of routes open to you to try to obtain payment. The best route to use depends on the specific circumstances and is something that you will need to discuss with your legal adviser.

The simplest approach may be to make a complaint to the Employment Appeals Tribunal alleging an unauthorised deduction from wages. The definition of wages covers both contractual and non-contractual bonuses. Such a claim must be made within three months of the deduction (or non-payment).

Another approach is to make a claim for breach of contract in the civil courts

Depending on the circumstances surrounding the redundancies, you may also have a claim for unfair dismissal (where the maximum compensatory award is 104 weeks gross remuneration). You should also be entitled to receive a statutory redundancy payment.

Can you claim for a promised review that never happened?

Last year you hired someone for your team. They were offered a salary greater than yours on the basis that you had received verbal confirmation from your boss that your salary would be reviewed and increased by the time that the new person actually started work. The review never happened, and the person has reported to you since joining at a higher salary than you. You have now been made redundant. Are you entitled to or likely to be able to claim for any compensation?

I will assume that you have worked for your employer prior to your dismissal for at least a year, in which case you have the right not be "unfairly dismissed".

After two years' service, you have the right to a statutory redundancy payment, although your company may make redundancy payments before two years' service, depending on the terms of its redundancy policy.

With regard to verbal confirmation that your salary would be reviewed and increased, your right to bring a claim depends on the certainty of what had been agreed between you and your employer. If you had been promised, even if only verbally, a performance review which did not happen, or a specific salary increase which has not been given, then you may be able to bring a claim for breach of contract in the civil courts or for unlawful deduction of wages at an Employment Appeals Tribunal but you must do the latter within six months of the end of your employment.

The difficulty you may have is that if you worked for a number of months after you should have received a salary increase, you may be seen to have accepted the breach.

Show me the money!

In addition, if the person who has been hired is of the opposite sex to you, you may have a claim under the equality legislation, which provides that men and women are entitled to equal pay for work that is the same or of a broadly similar nature; work rated as equivalent or work of an equal value to that of a person of the opposite sex. Any difference in pay must then be justified on grounds not related to sex.

In the circumstances, you may be entitled to claim an uplift in your salary from the date when the new person was hired and if you decide to bring a claim, it must be within six months of the end of your employment

If the person you hired received a non-contractual benefit (eg promotion or non-selection for redundancy), you may have an additional claim for sex discrimination, which you must bring before the end of a six-month period beginning with the discriminatory act complained of.

Negotiating a pay rise

You would like an increase in salary at your next pay review. You are not very skilled at asking for pay rises and usually accept less than you're happy with, and later regret it.

By way of preparation, you should be really clear about what you want specifically. What would you be delighted with, what would you be pleased with and what would you settle for?

You can, of course, include aspects other than remuneration such as pension, health benefits and company car.

Next prepare your case. What added value or contribution have you brought to your role? What makes you worth the extra? Seniority could also be a factor as could the going market rate for your role or additional responsibilities. Draw up a long list - this is not the time to be modest!

You'll have noticed the emphasis in **Smart Moves at Work** on presenting your case in a way that finance people will understand. The key point here is to make as much as you can quantifiable. For example, if the number of people you manage has increased from three to six, you could say that your management responsibilities have increased.

Alternatively you could state that they have doubled. You decide which would make the most impact.

Now choose only the **top three reasons** why you are worth more. Four is too many, two is too few. Somehow three always seems the right number. Watch how well-known people operate in the media (eg politicians being interviewed). They list things in threes.

It can be tempting to enter the negotiating room with as long a list as possible. This is a mistake professional negotiators soon learn to avoid. The weaker points you make can be picked off, one by one, and you could spend valuable time discussing minor aspects.

You should also avoid the, "...and another thing...and another reason", type of unhelpful dialogue that can be created when you make one point after another. So keep the focus on the three major reasons.

If your boss agrees and gives you what you wanted, congratulations. But what if the decision has been made and the answer is not to your satisfaction?

Now ask, "What would I need to do/ improve on/ produce/take responsibility for in order to get...?" "How long would I need to do that for? What would you advise me to do to accelerate it happening?

Get specific answers. From those answers you will have enough information to either plan your next steps or plan to move on.

Get ready for your annual performance review

Who honestly looks forward to their annual performance review? It must be the least loved of all management practices, right up there with submitting annual budgets for approval. Of course, everyone wants the feedback, but the thought of filling out all those forms or sitting through endless meetings can be a pain. It doesn't help that some employers continually 'improve' the process by changing it.

Really good managers don't spring surprises in the annual review; important feedback should be given contemporaneously. If you are managing other people, give them any feedback as the need for it arises, not 6 months later! Here are a few tips to help you prepare for your annual review.

Know your company's performance review system. To get the most from the experience and present yourself in the best light, make sure you understand how your company handles reviews, beginning with the form that has to be filled out.

Some companies ask employees to complete a self-review form, sometimes online. Others leave the writing to the boss and let employees have their say in a face-to-face meeting.

Incredible as it may seem, there are some employers that dispense with the face-to-face discussion and just dump the completed form on the employee's desk. If you are unlucky enough to work for one of these employers, consider whether it is time to start job hunting!

Record your progress during the year. Most performance-review systems operate on a yearly calendar. Keep track of your work throughout, so that you can cite your accomplishments. Keep a log, and review your e-mail regularly to refresh your memory on the projects, initiatives and challenges you've managed.

Your review notes should include:

- Your work over the past year, emphasising your above-the-norm contributions and initiatives

- Your goals for the next year

- What you need to do to achieve those goals, eg training and access to right people

- Your views on your own strengths and areas for improvement

- Any feedback for your boss, presuming he or she is someone who is open to suggestions.

Focus on your exceptional contributions, ie those that go beyond your normal duties and responsibilities. You will not automatically get a good review and a decent pay increase if you simply list everything you did during the year. You're *already paid* to do that work.

If you want a decent salary increase, then realise it is a reward for exceptional performance. So when you list your accomplishments, focus on the net value to the business. Remember what I said about presenting your case in a way that makes sense to financial and sales decision-makers (your managing director may be a sales person)? Make a case for your beyond-the-call-of-duty contributions. Just doing the job is not justification for an above-average review or pay increase.

If you have a compensation goal, say so. When a company has a widely known annual pay increase schedule (2% for average performance and 5% for excellent performance) and you make no comment prior to the review your manager will assume that you're happy with that. The review process in many multi-national and larger indigenous companies may not give you a chance to provide input on your pay. If you expect or want more than the standard, you have to make that clear in advance. This doesn't mean that you'll automatically get it. But asking for more may start a discussion that eventually will get you there.

Finally, let your manager know in advance the points you plan to raise. That way, you remove the 'I'll get back to you on that' excuse and can have a meaningful and useful discussion.

Finding a good recruitment firm

How do you pick a recruitment consultant and how many should you register with?

The first thing you should be aware of is the difference between a search firm and a recruitment agency.

Search firms traditionally have worked only on a mandated or exclusive basis. This means companies appoint a single search firm to fill specific posts, usually at a senior level. The posts are not advertised and the consultants make individual approaches to potential candidates. Search firms are increasingly taking on non-exclusive work as the market becomes more competitive and also because a number of the recruitment agencies now surpass them.

Recruitment agencies advertise vacancies on behalf of clients and then draw up a suitable shortlist. They deal with a broader range of positions from relatively junior upwards.

Because they deal with larger volumes of clients and vacancies, recruitment agencies tend to be more open to approaches from individual job seekers.

There are literally hundreds of recruitment agencies in Ireland with new companies springing up all the time. At the time of writing, a second wave of the Celtic Tiger economic boom is predicted and the recruiters are preparing for the huge fees they plan to harvest.

Take a careful look through the on-line jobs sites. Employers who use agencies tend to give the job specification to more than one agency, so you'll generally see the same role with at least two agencies.

Most agencies these days set themselves high standards. Some truly appalling agencies will fling the same role to a huge group of their ravenous recruiters, who will then battle it out to bring in the winning candidate. So, you might visit an on-line job site and think, great, there are 25 marketing director roles in an ideal location. All with the same agency too, what a useful coincidence! In fact, it turns out to be just one job. I suggest avoiding such agencies.

Have a chat with the agency and register with about three or four of those whom you like the best.

When you approach a search firm or a recruitment agency you should ask them to name their clients and try to get a sense of the nature of their relationships, the level of seniority of their contacts within their clients, and how long they have worked with them.

In either event, you should own the process from an administrative point of view - make sure that you do **not** have more than one search firm or recruitment agency approaching any one potential employer on your behalf.

Ultimately, it is the personal relationship that you develop with a consultant that will determine how useful their service is to you.

It is important to remember that if the consultant considers you to be a credible candidate then he or she will actively encourage his or her clients to interview you. Keep in regular contact with your recruitment consultant to let them know if you are still on the market.

Explaining a career break

You recently took a two-year break to undertake voluntary work abroad. Although you are able to be more committed to work than ever before you now feel awkward explaining your decision at interview, particularly since you've received a raft of rejections and recruitment consultants say employers think your actions shows a lack of commitment!

It's funny how different recruiters perceive the same thing in a different way. As a HR Director, I would have been quite impressed with your courage in leaving a permanent job and giving something back to society. I would be interested in hearing about the challenges you faced and how you overcame them. You might have some perceptive ideas on how an organisation could usefully address its corporate social responsibility aspirations.

And I'm sure that there is plenty of HR professionals and recruiters out there who would take a similar view. You'd still have to measure up to all the job and person requirements of course. And you'd need to be chomping at the bit to get back to work, just like any other keen candidate looking for a job.

In a very recent example, I've seen a person, with some seniority, who did leave his job in a commercial organisation in a planned way to work as a volunteer and who has found it to be a huge barrier to getting a job back in Ireland. Among the reasons given: "this looks like someone who will always want to break the mould"; "leaving a job shows a lack of commitment".

The advice given by recruiters? *'Change your CV to say that you took that time off to travel the world, much more acceptable'*. I want to say that this is shocking, but the truth is that in reality that part of old Ireland that still resents entrepreneurship continues to prevail in some companies; you'd get the same reaction if you were a self-employed person seeking to return to a permanent job.

Can a potential employer make you take a blood test?

You are about to start working for major multi-national. Prior to starting you have to go through a medical test. What is involved in such a test? Are they allowed to draw blood?

Most potential recruits for senior, highly paid positions are required to undertake some form of pre-employment medical examination. Equally, candidates for jobs in call centres and factories are required to attend medicals. So the chances are, most candidates will face a medical at some point.

These examinations are generally of a relatively cursory nature, involving a short questionnaire being completed, blood pressure being taken and a brief physical examination. The candidate may be asked to undertake sight and hearing tests. You may disclose some medical condition to the doctor that he or she does not consider relevant to your medical fitness to do the job, in which case the doctor is highly unlikely to disclose it.

In most areas of employment, a blood test would not normally be required. An exception would be where the employer was providing a very high value life insurance premium; in this case the insurer might require a full-scale medical including a blood test. If you are in this category, then you'll be earning so much that a medical won't worry you!

Otherwise a blood test would only be undertaken with a view to analysing a specific condition or testing for evidence of recreational drugs. It is possible that in certain sectors, eg on a trading floor or other banking activities involving large funds, an employer may wish to screen employees for drug usage.

Clearly the potential employer will only be allowed to draw blood with your consent. However, it is possible that a refusal to undertake a blood test would result in a job offer being withdrawn. A possible exception to this would be if you could demonstrate the existence of a genuine phobia concerning needles.

It would be potentially discriminatory for an employer to require only disabled applicants to undergo a medical examination, if the nature of their disability did not give rise to any specific potential medical concern in the context of the working environment.

Legislation providing for random testing for intoxicants is being proposed for Irish rail workers, though trade unions believe that it is unconstitutional. Such testing is already in place for military personnel and workers employed by Dublin's new tram system, LUAS.

Drug testing has been making steady inroads into Irish workplaces over the past decade or so. However, most of it is still confined to pre-employment screening and legal questions remain over random mandatory testing, which is confined to the Defence Forces and Dublin's LUAS new light rail operation, as well as some private sector organisations.

The pre-employment agreement between SIPTU and Connex, the operator of Dublin's new LUAS tram service, provides for random testing. Cooperation with such testing is a condition of employment and the testing is to be done on 'a random, fair basis, with proper respect for the employee's privacy and rights'.

How can you find companies looking for non-executive directors?

Most directorships in Ireland are based on business or personal contacts. Keep in mind that being a director entails considerable responsibility these days, so much so that senior people are becoming somewhat less inclined to take on these roles.

I recommend that you read up on directors' duties and responsibilities. You'll find information from the following sources:

Companies Registration Office
www.cro.ie

Office of Director of Corporate Enforcement
www.odce.ie

Department of Enterprise and Employment
www.entemp.ie

Centre for Corporate Governance (UCD and Institute of Directors)
http://www.ucd.ie/corpgov/

The business pages of the daily and weekend newspapers also discuss corporate compliance on a regular basis.

You could also spend plenty of time on the golf course, where a lot of networking takes place!

How creative can you be with your CV?

A recruitment consultant has suggested that you change the details on your CV to match the requirements of job you are interested in. It's to make you more marketable, but is it legal?

It all depends what you are being asked to alter! It is perfectly acceptable to tailor a CV to a particular job by placing the emphasis on different elements of your skills and experience to match the requirements of a potential new job.

This is not dishonesty, but a sensible way of marketing yourself properly.

What is *not* acceptable is to deliberately distort or invent information. If you falsify information on your CV, you are likely to be found out. This will result in the offer being withdrawn, or summary dismissal for gross misconduct if that information doesn't come to light until after you've started in the job. This would be extremely damaging to your career. In extreme cases it could even result in legal action against you. You wouldn't have a leg to stand on.

Deliberate lies in a CV or application, about salary or anything else, is fraud, and there is no ethical, moral or practical justification for it.

Discovery of dishonesty in an application process will normally result in instant dismissal.

I would advise you never to let anyone persuade you to include anything on your CV that is not true. By all means redraft your CV whenever necessary to emphasise those parts of your background most relevant to the position you are applying for.

But **never, ever put false dates** on your CV, even if you are inclined to do so because you can't remember your exact start or leaving date. A certain amount of reference checking is outsourced. If your dates don't match those held by a former employer, your reference will come back rejected.

You've just had one employer. Is this a disadvantage?

You have been with the same company for 10 years, in different roles. During this time, your employer has merged with another company. Now you would like to leave and find a new job but it seems to be a disadvantage, especially with recruitment agencies. What can you do?

I can think of several employers who would love to see more candidates with this length of service.

The main reason you may encounter some resistance from recruitment agencies is that they are wondering whether you will really leave and start a new job. They do like to see a fairly speedy financial return for their efforts.

The trick here is to re-draft your CV so that each position looks like a different job. You should also demonstrate, if you can, how your career has progressed during this 10 year period: what you have achieved, what you have learnt, how you have coped with and adapted to changes brought on by this merger.

Look objectively at how you present yourself at interview too. Is there any danger that you could be perceived as being a little set in your ways, a creature of habit, someone who will not transplant well? Or are you keen and looking for a new challenge? Wanting to bring your extensive skills to a new company and make a difference?

If your details are forwarded to a potential new employer, find out something about them that is different to what you've experienced and mention at interview how you would relish this.

Ask yourself why you want to leave your employer and find a new job. Although the trend is to move every few years, if you are lucky enough to have a job and employer you really enjoy, there is nothing wrong with staying put.

How do references work?

Are they meant to stress your good points, give an honest opinion or can the employer say anything they want? Can an employee see their reference to ascertain the level of accuracy? If not, what steps can an employee take against an unfair reference?

References can be a very controversial issue. Employment legislation, employment tribunal rulings, the Data Protection Act and even financial services regulations all affect what employers can or can't do, or should or shouldn't do.

Generally HR departments write references. Prospective employers will normally ask for two satisfactory references. A personal reference from a boss who is familiar with your work is ideal, but most prospective employers realise that referees often give generic references.

Employers in Ireland are not required by law to provide references, although financial and medical services employers do have a legal obligation to disclose certain facts should a former employee have breached certain rules or acted improperly.

In practice, many employers will not do more than confirm basic details such as your job-title and dates employed. Employers are sometimes reluctant to give references, because by doing so they expose themselves to a potential liability. This is because when providing a reference, an employer owes a duty of care (both to the party to whom the reference is provided and to yourself, as the subject of reference) to provide a true, accurate and fair reference that does not give a misleading impression.

There have been legal cases in the UK brought against former employers who have given inaccurate or negative references.

Should a former employee feel that a reference is inaccurate, they have the right under the Data Protection Act to see a copy of the reference. If they have suffered any loss as a result, they are entitled to seek redress and compensation at an Employment Appeals Tribunal or in court. Redress also applies to verbal references.

You've been offered a new job, but you're pregnant

You have just been offered a new job and have discovered that you are pregnant. Do you have to tell your prospective new employer and can they withdraw their offer?

You are under no obligation to notify your prospective new employer that you are pregnant. Indeed, you'd suspect the motives of an employer who asked such a question about pregnancy and future family intentions. Though it happens. In interviews for two senior Human Resource positions I was asked when I planned to become pregnant in one and told categorically in another "there'll be no getting married!" I ignored the comment on both occasions, was offered and took up both jobs.

My motivation was that such an environment would be a huge challenge for a HR director, and it both cases it was! So how you react can depend on the type of job role. In most positions, I would suggest running a mile from such a company.

In your case, your potential employer would be on very thin ice indeed if they were to withdraw their offer as a result of your pregnancy. The European Court of Justice established some time ago that such a refusal is direct discrimination in breach of the Equal Treatment Directive.

Similarly, if you can prove that your offer of employment is withdrawn as a result of your pregnancy, this would be a breach of the Maternity Protection Act, 1994, which prohibits dismissal on the grounds of pregnancy. In addition, the Employment Equality Act, 1998, prohibits discrimination on the grounds of family status (and eight other grounds). Your case would be strengthened because you would not have to compare your situation with that of a male applicant, merely prove that the withdrawal of the offer was because of your pregnancy.

Having established this, the employer will have no defence. As pointed out earlier, you would have to show that your offer of employment was withdrawn because of your pregnancy. The only circumstance where an employer might have a defence is if you have been offered a job on a fixed-term contract and your absence due to pregnancy would mean that you would be unavailable for the whole of the work for which you had been engaged. An example would be where the work is of a purely seasonal duration, eg packing shamrock for St Patrick's Day.

You were fired during your 6 months probationary period. Should you tell your new employer?

Is it wise to tell employers that you were on a 6-month contract that was not extended or should you stick to the truth?

Which is the truth? That you were on a fixed-term 6-month contract that ended? Fixed-term contracts come to an end, by definition.

Or were you were in a permanent job with a 6-month probation period that ended unsuccessfully?

You might be asked in future interviews whether you would have liked to continue with that employer. Answer truthfully and in a businesslike manner. Some like, *"that particular role came to an end because ...... but it is a good company, in particular I like..."* The more businesslike you are about this, the more accepting your listener will be. You don't have to commit a crime not to pass your probationary period. Sometimes a new hire is put in the wrong job and that's all there is to it.

I suggest that you ask your last employer for a reference which talks about your good points as well as the reason for your termination. Unless you have done something terrible, this shouldn't usually be a problem.

Both on a practical as well as on a moral basis, always, always tell the truth about the reasons for termination. Most employers will take references, particularly for short-term employment. People who lie will never be hired, or if discovered later, are frequently fired.

Although you will naturally feel worried, you will get this tricky issue out of the way and can forget about it. Plenty more fish in the sea!

Should you resign to job hunt?

You are currently employed as a funds accountant and would consider handing in your resignation to have more time for your job search. Could interviewers perceive such a move negatively?

Take it as guaranteed that an interviewer would view such a move negatively! You are always perceived to be in a stronger bargaining and negotiating position whilst still employed.

A job search can be a somewhat time consuming and distracting process. However, if you have a targeted and systematic approach and enlist the help of a select number of reputable recruitment consultants you should be able to manage your current role and job search in tandem.

Believe it or not, you'll also make better use of your time. If you are unaccustomed to working from home, it takes time to adjust to the discipline that is needed to treat your home-based work as a proper job. Even at that, you will not need to spend all day every day searching for a job.

Another compelling reasons for staying in your job is that you will not have an income if you leave. If you leave a job voluntarily, you can't claim for unemployment benefit immediately. If you do leave and can't claim, you should still 'sign on' for PRSI credits, otherwise you'll break the continuity of your PRSI records.

Finally, you'll create an unnecessary question mark over why you are unemployed. To be honest, you'll also raise a question about how smart you really are.

Not really a great idea to resign just yet, is it? Take a holiday instead!

Should you be honest about your health?

You are currently between roles, having worked in operational management roles for 8 years. Although you are fairly fit, you suffer from a chronic health problem that means that you cannot put in the long hours that you used to. You want to be open about your problem in interviews. Is this a mistake?

It is never a mistake to be open and honest about health issues at interview. However, it may be wiser to disclose this at a later stage of the selection process, perhaps at offer stage.

The Employment Equality Act applies to job applicants as well as employees, and it could therefore be illegal for an offer to be withdrawn in these circumstances. The reaction of your interviewer might reveal a lot about the company's core values.

Of course, many employers require you to complete a written application form, irrespective of whether you have submitted a CV. Finding out this kind of information is one of the reasons for the application form. You must complete this form honestly, though be very clear about whether this disability affects your ability to do the job or just to work excessive hours.

An alternative strategy would be to offer your services as a part-time employee either on a direct basis, or through a recruitment agency.

Working as a contractor could also suit you, as you could take contracts for a quite a short time and then take a short break?

You can find out more about contracting in my books *Go Contracting in Ireland* and *Go Contracting in the UK.*

See www.smartmovesatwork.com

Will a stutter harm your career chances?

You would like to go into financial services or the technology sector when you graduate but you are concerned about your speech impediment - you have a stutter. Would this hinder your chances of being employed?

Well, a stutter hasn't held back Proinsios de Rossa, has it? A TD for years, he is now an MEP, appears regularly in the media, stutters occasionally; it doesn't seem to bother him and very few people really notice. That's because media interviewers and the public in general are used to it, just as your future employer will become accustomed to your speech impediment. It makes absolutely no difference to what the man says.

And what about the ebullient broadcaster Jonathan Ross, who has an unusual way with the letter 'r'? He delights in being challenged to say "*r*iding in a *R*olls *R*oyce is *r*eally *r*idiculous" for instance; he charmingly turns what could be seen as a 'problem' into an asset.

It is worth remembering that any potential employer should be assessing your competence and technical ability and not your physiological state. There are many opportunities within financial services and in IT in which a speech impediment should be irrelevant to your ability to do the job.

These are typically less client facing roles, such as back office administration, the full spectrum of research roles across all product areas and more execution orientated roles within corporate finance. In IT, there is a broad range of product development opportunities and even technical support, a great deal of which is now web-based.

Before you go to any interviews, preparation is vital. This is sound advice for anyone seeking employment in a competitive field but it is particularly important for you, especially if your stutter is exacerbated by stressful situations like job interviews.

Getting a job

Research the job and the employer thoroughly. Make sure that you are as confident as you can be about your skills and competencies. Do practice interviews, either at your career's service, or even by applying for jobs that you are less interested in.

Your aim is to show any potential employer that you are an outstanding candidate. Your speech impediment will not stop you doing a great job, will it? Didn't think so.

You are being interviewed in an unstructured way with no reference to job requirements

You've encountered a **gut-feeling** interview. This is an unstructured interview with little or no reference to job requirements, where the interviewer relies on their gut feeling or intuition and on whether or not they like you. Gut-feeling interviewers tend to subscribe to "pet theories". For example, they might ask you questions about what type of sports you have played, because they believe that playing contact sports builds competitiveness.

An interviewer who relies on their instincts about you will often be looking for your similarities to themselves. If he is someone who has had to fight his way to the top, he might ask you if you are confrontational (by which he means assertive and able to influence), perceiving this as positive assertiveness. This example illustrates how the arbitrary nature of unstructured interviews can disadvantage the candidate.

Another disadvantage of unstructured interviews is that the interviewer can form an opinion in the first few minutes and then spend the remaining time justifying his gut reaction. I advise against this kind of interviewing as it may lead to discrimination.

You can't control the way the interviewer conducts the interview but you can control your own responses. Once you have prepared for interview with a series of responses to about twenty scenarios you will be well equipped to direct the conversation in a more constructive way. You'll find 21-interview question strategies, and sample questions later in this section of *Smart Moves at Work.*

Your interviewer seems to think you're there for a friendly chat and has not prepared any interview questions

This approach is an unstructured interview focusing mainly on job experience and job skills. There is no prepared list of questions and the conversation will usually flow naturally from one topic to another, similar to a social situation. Although this may seem likely a friendly chat, the conversational interviewer is using rapport rather than structure to gain information.

The intention is to make you feel comfortable, and therefore perhaps more likely to reveal information than you may otherwise have felt reluctant to mention. It is absolutely fine for you to behave informally in this situation; however, maintain your professionalism and give plenty of examples about yourself and your colleagues, rather than using generalisations.

It would be a mistake to treat this kind of interview as easier than others, although it may seem to be. A good conversational interviewer is using a clever technique to get you to open up. Provided you are aware of the technique and have prepared your **21 questions** you can turn this to your own advantage by leading the conversation yourself through the examples and topics that you introduce to illustrate your own skills. As with all interviews, you cannot control the questions, but you can control the way in which you answer those questions.

What are your three greatest strengths and weaknesses?

(the dumbest question ever asked at interview)

As a HR professional, I think this is a real cop-out question for someone who is not comfortable with interviewing. But there are plenty of people who have had absolutely no interview training and so consider this question a safe bet. You may agree with me, but will gain nothing from pointing this out to your interviewer, so don't! Also, don't laugh out loud if he asks it.

One reason I think this is a silly question is that all human beings have strengths and weaknesses. What smart person is going to tell an interviewer their bad points?

Secondly, what relationship does this 'information' have to do with how you match with the job requirements or with your ability to do the job? There is very little measurable connection!

Thirdly, what smart interviewer will ask a question, the answer to which could leave him open to a discrimination claim later?

Nonetheless, you'll be asked the strengths/weaknesses question at some point, generally in a **trait interview**. Trait interviews are person-related and may or may not be structured. You will be asked questions that relate more to your personal characteristics than your job skills, sometimes without reference to the kind of work to be done.

So yes, a typical question would be: "What are your three greatest strengths and weaknesses/areas for development?" You should prepare for this question by identifying a list of your positive characteristics; for example, "I enjoy working on projects with other people". When you cite your negative traits, do so in a positive light, for example: "It bothers me when others do not pull their weight in meeting a deadline." Then follow up with a specific example of a time you put this particular positive trait into practice.

Keep in mind, if you do fall into the trap of listing 3 each of your strengths and weaknesses, you'll sound like an old-fashioned Catholic confession: "and here are 3 of my sins......"

Although experts acknowledge that trait interviews, if combined with personality tests and carried out by well-trained interviewers, can produce accurate results, the pitfall from the candidate's perspective is that a trait (characteristic) can become a label that reflects an impression rather than actual information.

For example, one well-known stereotype is to classify an assertive, confident male as "decisive", a similar female as "bossy". Classifying an everyday task such as cooking as something that women do has the reverse effect; a person who thinks this way may consider men who like cooking to be feeble.

The downside for the interviewer is that a practised candidate can perform well at interview and give all the right answers without having to give specific examples from their past actions.

Again, be prepared for this scenario by having your 21-interview questions strategies in order.

What is a competency-based interview?

Competency based (or behavioural) interviews are based on the premise that past behaviour is the best predictor of future behaviour.

Interviewers seek to obtain information about candidates' past behaviour in certain situations. Competency based interviews are structured, with questions that relate directly to the essential criteria/ competencies required for the post.

Research into recruitment and selection methodology suggests that structured, competency based interviews can be one of the most reliable and accurate forms of assessment.

A good recruitment and selection interview should assess candidates against each essential criteria or competency, asking questions about:

> Past behaviours and performance
> Learning from past behaviours
> Future adaptability to new position
> Knowledge and understanding of issues in relation to the position

Note to untrained interviewers: this doesn't mean leaping to conclusions. Ask questions relating to the competencies required for the job and accept the answer given in that context.

What does the interview focus on?
Most interviews will focus on six key areas. These will mostly be competencies, but may also include other knowledge-based essential criteria.

They will be focused on those competencies that are most important for the particular job.

Getting a job

You may also be required to meet other, specific essential criteria. This could be an in-depth knowledge of a particular area or experience of working in a similar role previously.

What should you expect in the Interview?

Competency based interview questions may be slightly different to the style you may be used to. They will tend to focus on past situations and your behaviour in those situations.

Questions are likely to start with:

"Please give me an example when. . ." or "Please describe an occasion"

What will the interviewers be looking for?

The interviewers will be looking for **specific examples about exactly what you did** in such situations, not what the team's role as a whole was, or what you would do in a hypothetical situation.

You can choose to use relevant examples from your current job, a previous role, or a situation outside of work altogether. You will be asked to discuss the example in some detail.

It is likely that the interviewers will then follow with some probing questions, possibly clarifying a particular area. They will be interested in the outcome of the situation, whether there was anything you learned from the experience.

The interviewers may also want to ask you questions about the information you have provided in your application form. So, read through your application form again.

Look again at the essential requirements of the job, as outlined in the advertisement. If you want a more detailed job or person spec, ask if one is available. The interviewers will ask questions related to those requirements. Try to anticipate what questions may be asked.

As the interview will be focused on past specific examples, it is essential to think about possible examples that you could use.

Oh no, wrong answer!

You always leave interviews regretting the way you've answered the questions. How can you prevent this happening in future?

Although you will not know in advance the kind of style your interviewer will adopt, you can greatly enhance your chances of success by thorough preparation. Having made a list of your different skills using the sample questions above, you need to structure your answers. Preparing for a competency-based interview should equip you for any interview. Your golden rule should be to **back up what ever you say with examples of when you used specific skills**.

The SHARE technique is an excellent guide for preparing your examples in a way that will best illustrate your skills and experience. A SHARE answer provides specific information on the situation, hindrances, actions, results and evaluation.

Situation: Describe the situation in which you were operating.

Hindrances: Describe any constraints/hindrances to your actions.

Actions: Explain exactly what you did.

Results: Describe the results that can be attributed to your actions.

Evaluation: Summarise the evaluation with a positive example of your skill.

Now work on your 21-interview questions strategies to prepare yourself for any interview. You may surprise yourself at how skilled you are. Having prepared in this way will leave you feeling much more confident on the day.

21 interview questions strategies

As you cannot expect to predict exactly which company uses which technique, the best approach is to prepare thorough answers of a range of **job- and skills-based questions** that you can use at every interview, **using real examples in your answers**.

Using the SHARE technique described earlier, in preparation for interview, ask yourself and be prepared to answer the following questions. These examples highlight some of the skills that interviewers look for. The skills required for every job differ, so try putting yourself in the interviewer's position and try to think of questions you might pose relating to your particular job to gain evidence of each of the listed skills.

1.   Confirm details on your CV/ application form: why you made certain choices at different times, such as choice of education, job, why you are looking for a new job. This is an opportunity to show that you are someone who can think things through. Without appearing to be an extreme planner, be ready to illustrate how you have used reasonable and logical thinking when making decisions that have had an impact on your life.

2.   Interpersonal skills: give simple, everyday examples to illustrate that you can build different kinds of relationships with other people and that you are aware of their feelings and opinions. Think of examples that show your flexibility in interacting with others. The importance of these skills cannot be stressed too strongly.

3.   Describe situations where you had to deal with stress: questions may be posed about meeting a deadline, dealing with an angry person, dealing with conflict where the conflict concerns you. The interviewer is looking for evidence of your coping skills.

4. **Ability to cope with change**: give an example where you had to deal with the unexpected at work. Think carefully about this; perhaps you could cite an example where you had to resolve *not to do something* because of changing circumstances. Here, **evidence of your skills in dealing with and tolerating unclear and unstructured situations is required**.

5. **Acting decisively**: be ready to describe situations where you have had to act quickly, make unpopular decisions, put contingency plans into place, keep to decisions.

6. **Decision-making/problem-solving**: this is not the same skill as being decisive, where the speed with which you take action is a skill. Here the interviewer is looking for your ability to understand issues and use reason and good judgement. As you think of your examples, consider to what extent emotion guided your decision. If you have examples of where you have displayed creativity in solving problems, use them.

7. Listen carefully to the questions. If the interviewer asks you about having to **accept an unpopular decision**, they are looking for a different skill to decision-making, such as the **ability to accept company culture**.

8/9. **Verbal and written communication**: two distinct skills important for all jobs, particularly those involving leadership. The interviewer is seeking evidence that you possess listening skills, can speak and write clearly, and can influence others. Think of examples in both positive and negative situations. The question may be phrased in a number of different ways, depending on the context. For example, be aware that if you are asked about having to be assertive, it is worth mentioning times when you succeeded in being **tactfully assertive** when you select an example.

10. You may be asked if you ever had to **follow a set of written instructions.** Be careful on this one. It is surprising how many candidates reply "no", although they may have just completed written aptitude tests with instructions on how to complete each part.

11. Leading and Motivating: think of examples where you had a motivating effect on others. It could be in any situation, not just work. This skill is desired in employees at all levels, not just managers, and your answer merits good preparation. This is also a good opportunity to include examples of when you have recognised the contributions of colleagues and others, which is evidence of motivational ability in itself.

Remember too that competition can motivate, so the interviewer is not looking for examples that emphasise purely soft skills.

12. If you are interviewing for a leadership position, the interviewer is probably also looking for evidence of your **ability to evaluate objectively.**

13. Following the party line: be ready to describe situations where you had to follow, implement or explain company policies and procedures. Every job and company has some routine, established procedures. Nobody will hire someone who wants to reinvent the wheel every time. Equally, as a leader you will be called on to implement with conviction decisions you do not agree with, as though they were your own.

Try to think of some real examples in your response to this question.

14. Another related skill is your **ability to understand the corporate and organisational culture** and recognise where and when you can use this to achieve goals. For example, you may have found that before making an important presentation, it helped to talk individually and informally to your audience in advance to individually gain their support.

15. **Alertness**: think of examples where you were prepared and alert in a normal everyday working environment. Although quick thinking is part of this skill, it is not the same as being decisive.

Being alert is being proactive, displaying decisiveness, and reacting. The interviewer is looking for examples of how alert you are, whether or not you are on the ball.

This is a question that you would particularly expect to be asked in a manufacturing environment, where changes in the physical surroundings where machinery is being used can have a major impact.

However, your examples need not be high level. For example, you are responsible for ensuring that your team's weekly overtime hours are communicated to payroll and you notice an hour before the payroll cut-off that your neighbouring team leader is absent through illnesses. Without being asked, you take steps to ensure that his or her team gets paid. You're on the ball.

16. **Solving problems using analysis**: give examples of when you had to make an informed decision based on a range of possible solutions. This question will not be asked for every job, but many positions do involve the use of analytical tools to some extent. Think of any examples that involve using maths at any level.

17.   Setting goals and objectives: for yourself and others, prioritising workload, time management. Evidence of initiative and logic should feature in your response.

18.   Planning work: a valid question for many jobs. Everyone has examples of organising and if you have better examples from your life outside work, then use them. This point is often brought home when teamwork is introduced in companies, only to find that many of the members of the production teams have already held managerial responsibilities in their sports and leisure activities.

19.   Showing commitment: think of examples where you had to work extra hours or give up leisure time because you were committed to achieving something, or perhaps stuck with something boring until it was complete. You should not limit your examples to work situations. Remember that working long hours *every day* may raise questions about your organisational ability in many companies.

20.   Team building: evidence is being sought of your ability to work with other people in a way that builds morale and contributes to the team/group meeting its goals. Give real examples of where you contributed to planning and meeting group goals, were able to step back and allow someone else complete a desirable task or be the spokesperson, even if you wanted to assume the role yourself. This is a good opportunity to illustrate that you have learned new skills.

21.   Technical skills. Be clear about what you do know and what you do not. If you have applied for a job that requires any kind of technical knowledge, be prepared to answer detailed questions about this area. Make sure you are up to date, or at least aware of, new developments in your field.

Sample Interview Questions

1. Tell me about a time when you displayed excellent customer service?

2. What has given you the greatest sense of achievement at work? Why?

3. All jobs have frustration; can you describe some aspects of your job, which frustrate you? Careful! Don't use the word 'frustrating' in your answer. Talk about the 'challenges', the steps you took to meet them (remember the SHARE technique for answering interview questions) and how much you relish challenge. If you don't like challenge all the time and are being interviewed for a job steeped in routine, then adjust your message accordingly.

4. What standards have you set for yourself in your current position? How well have you done in terms of meeting these standards?

5. Can you provide me with 3 situations in which you did not succeed and why? Remember the '3 sins' trap! Try to select an example to which a credible reason for the lack of success can be found. If you made some mistake early on in your career, by all means admit to it and then move on to explain how you learned from it, as illustrated by this example ...and then outline the example that shows you didn't repeat the mistake the next time you were faced with similar circumstances.

6. Have you ever introduced a new idea? Can you describe what it covered, the steps you took to implement it and why you saw the need to introduce it? No need to limit

your answer to just one example here. Use the SHARE technique to outline at least one very good example.

7. Tell me a time when you were confronted with an unexpected problem? How did you deal with it? What happened? Again, have more than one example ready.

8. Tell me about a time when you had to go above and beyond the call of duty in getting a job done.

9. Give me an example of a time when you were able to successfully communicate to another person even when that individual may not have personally liked you (or you them). Again, be **very careful**. You might appear to reflect for a few moments and then say you can't think of an example where *dislike* was involved but you do have a good example where you didn't *know* the person very well/ the person didn't know you very well. Then give *that* example. That's a smart move.

10. Can you describe a time when you dealt with a difficult person? How did you handle it and what happened?

11. Can you give an example of a deadline you have had to meet?

12. Describe a situation in which you were able to use persuasion to successfully convince someone to see things your way.

13. Describe an instance when you had to think on your feet to disentangle yourself from a difficult situation.

14. Give me a specific example of a time when you used good judgment and logic in solving a problem.

15. By providing examples, convince me that you can adapt to a wide variety of people, situations, and environments.

16. Describe a time in any job that you have held in which you were faced with problems and stresses that tested your coping skills.

17. Tell me about a time in which you had to use your written communication skills in order to get an important point across.

18. Describe a specific occasion in which you conformed to a policy with which you did not agree.

19. Give me an example of an important goal that you had set in the past and tell me your success in reaching it.

20. Describe the most significant or creative presentation that you have had to compose.

21. Has there been a time when you improved a process? What was it? How did you go about making the changes (step by step)? Be ready to answer in detail such questions as "what were you thinking at that point?" or "tell me more about meeting with that person", or "lead me through your decision process".

Remember, these are not trick questions. There are no right or wrong answers. The interviewer is trying to predict how you might act in similar situations in the future by asking you to decide how you have acted in the past.

If you are unclear about a question, ask for clarification. Take your time to answer it completely. As the interview progresses, if you feel there is something you want to add, then say so.

Your interviewers will be taking notes. If it helps you, it's fine for you to jot a few notes down; just don't let it distract you.

The most important point is to prepare plenty of real examples, think them out in advance and you'll then have those responses ready to draw on no matter what question you are asked.

Again, I stress the importance of not jumping to conclusions. As an employer, you may have observed someone at his or her worst. That doesn't mean he or she would respond in the same way if faced with those circumstances again. Make sure you know all of the facts before reaching a conclusion. The surest way to do that is by asking them.

Please feel free to post your comments about your workplace and interview experiences on my 'blog' at this website www.smartmovesatwork.com

You want to learn to sell effectively

No matter what your job is, it is a smart move to learn effective sales skills and, of course, to use them. For the purposes of this section, I am assuming that you want sales skills so that you can sell as part of your job. This may mean direct responsibility for generating sales revenue, or it could be that you need to submit tender documents or requests for funding. Even if you think 'I could never sell', do read this section carefully to see how you can apply good sales skills to enhance your career prospects.

Forecasting and planning your sales

Accurately forecasting your sales and building a sales plan can help you to avoid unforeseen cash flow problems and manage your production, staff and financing needs more effectively.

A sales forecast is an essential tool for managing a business of any size. It is a month-by-month forecast of the level of sales you expect to achieve. Most businesses draw up a sales forecast once a year.

Equipped with this information you can rapidly identify problems and opportunities - and do something about them.

While it's always wise to expect the unexpected, a well-constructed sales plan, combined with accurate sales forecasting, can allow you to spend more time developing your business rather than responding to day-to-day developments in sales and marketing.

Sales forecasts enable you to manage your business more effectively. Before you begin, here are a few questions that may help clarify your position:

- How many new customers do you gain each year?
- How many customers do you lose each year?
- What is the average level of sales you make to each customer?

- Are there particular months where you win or lose more customers than usual?

Existing businesses

The starting point for your sales forecast is last year's sales.

Before you factor in a new product launch, or economic trend, look at the level of sales for each customer last year. Do you know of any customers who are going to buy more - or less - from you next year?

In the case of customers who account for a significant value of sales, you may want to ask them if they plan to change their purchase level in the foreseeable future.

New businesses

New businesses have to make assumptions based on market research and good judgement.

Every business can also add in the new customers that it expects to win without actually knowing who they are, or what they will buy. Simply enter "new customer" on your forecast.

Depending on your type of business, you may want to specify the volume of sales in the forecast - for example, how many two-litre cans of paint you sell - as well as the value of sales. By knowing the volume, you can plan the necessary resources in areas such as production, storage and transport.

Your sales assumptions

Every year is different so you need to list any changing circumstances that could significantly affect your sales. These factors - known as the sales forecast assumptions - form the basis of your forecast.

Wherever possible, put a figure against the change - as shown in the examples below. You can then get a feel for the impact it will have on your business. Also, give the reasoning behind each figure, so that other people can comment on whether it's realistic. Here are some **typical assumptions**:

The market

The market you sell into will grow by two per cent.
Your market share will shrink by two per cent, due to the success of a competitor.

Your resources

You will double your sales force from three people to six people, halfway through the year.
You will spend 50 per cent less on advertising, which will reduce sales of your product.

Overcoming barriers to sale

You are moving to a better location, which will lead to 30 per cent more customers buying next year.
You are raising prices by 10 per cent, which will reduce the volume of products sold by 5 per cent but result in a 4.5 per cent increase in overall revenue.

Your products

Are you launching any new products? Sales may be small to begin with.
Which products are newly established? Is there potential to increase sales rapidly?
Which products enjoy steady sales but have little growth potential?
Which products face declining sales, perhaps because of a competitor's superior product?

For new businesses, the assumptions need to be based on market research and good judgement.

Developing your forecast

Start by writing down your sales assumptions. You can then create your sales forecast. This becomes easy once you've found a way to break the forecast down into individual items.

- Can you break down your sales by product, market, or geographic region?

- Are individual customers important enough to your business to warrant their own individual sales forecast?

- Can you estimate the conversion rate - the percentage chance of the sale happening - for each item on your sales forecast? For example, you might predict that a customer will purchase €1000 worth of products. If you estimate that there's a 70 per cent chance of this customer purchasing, the forecast sales for this customer are €700, ie 70 per cent of €1000.

Selling more of your product to an existing customer is far easier than making a first sale to a new customer. So the conversion rates for existing customers are much higher than those for new customers.

You may want to include details of which product each customer will probably buy. Then you can spot potential problems. One product could sell out, whilst another might not shift at all.

By predicting actual sales, you're forecasting what you think will be sold. This is generally far more accurate than forecasting from a target figure and then trying to work out how to achieve it.

The completed sales forecast isn't just used to plan and monitor your sales efforts. It's also a vital part of the cash flow.

Avoiding forecasting pitfalls

Five common forecasting pitfalls are:

1.   Wishful thinking

It's all too easy to be over-optimistic. It's a good idea to look back at the previous year's forecast to see if your figures are realistic. New businesses should avoid the mistake of working out the level of sales they need for the business to be viable, then putting this figure in as the forecast.

Is it physically possible to achieve the sales levels you're forecasting? For example:

- One taxi can only make a certain number of airport trips each day
- A factory can only manufacture a given amount of products on each shift
- A sales team can only visit a certain number of customers each week

2.   Ignoring your own assumptions

Make sure your sales assumptions are linked to the detailed sales forecast; otherwise you can end up with completely contradictory information. For instance, if you assume a declining market and declining market share, then it's illogical to forecast increased sales.

3.   Moving goalposts

Make sure the forecast is finalised and agreed within a set time scale. If you're spending a lot of time refining the forecast, it can distract you from focusing on your targets. Avoid changing the detail of the forecast, even if you discover it's too optimistic or pessimistic.

4.   Failure to consult

Your sales people probably have the best knowledge of your customers' buying intentions, therefore:

> Ask for their opinions
> Give them time to ask their customers about this
> Get the sales team's agreement to their targets

5.   Lack of feedback

Having built your sales forecast, you need someone to challenge it. Get someone experienced to review the whole document.

You want to learn to sell effectively

Creating a sales plan

The questions you should answer in your sales plan are:

1. What are you going to focus on?
2. What are you going to change?
3. In practical terms, what steps are involved?
4. What territories and targets are you going to give each salesperson or team?

The sales plan will start with some strategic objectives. Here are some examples:

> Break into the public sector market by adapting your product for this market
>
> Open a shop in an area that you believe has the potential for generating lots of sales
>
> Boost the average sale per customer

You can then explain the stepping-stones that will allow you to achieve these objectives. Use objectives that are **SMART - Specific, Measurable, Achievable, Realistic, Time-specific.**

Using the example of breaking into the public sector market, the stepping stones might be:

1. By end January, hire a sales person with experience of the public sector market on a salary of €50,000 with OTE (on target earnings) of €120,000
2. Fully train the sales person by mid March
3. Ensure that any changes the product development team has agreed to make are ready to pilot by the beginning of March

4. As well as planning for new products and new markets, explain how you're going to improve sales and profit margins for your existing products and markets.

It is often helpful to think how you remove barriers to sales.

1. Can you increase the activity levels of the sales team - more telephone calls per day, or more customer visits per week?
2. Can you increase the conversion rate of calls into sales - through better sales training or better sales support materials?

You want to target the right people in a potential client organisation

To make a sale, you need to know how to identify and make contact with the key decision-makers in other businesses

When you're selling to other businesses, you need to pinpoint and then target the decision-makers. Don't waste time selling to someone who doesn't have the power to buy your product or service.

The main decision-maker is often the individual who signs the cheque - but this won't always be the only person you need to convince. Others may also play an important role in the buying process.

People involved in the buying process

There are at least three stages in a buying decision and the power to buy your product or service won't always rest with just one person:

The *influencer* is a key user of the product, perhaps a manager of a department.

The *specifier* draws up the requirement, often led by the influencer.

A *final decision-maker* has the authority to agree or veto a deal and to sign the cheque.

So when you're selling to other businesses, you need to identify who these people are and keep them all on board. If these responsibilities are held by one person your job may be easier.

The smart move is to aim as high up the chain as you can. So if you've discovered that it's the managing director who'll sign the cheque for your product, that's who you need to call.

The person at the top of the chain will probably put you through to the influencer or specifier or ask you to send them an email or letter. But at least the ultimate decision-maker will be aware of your presence.

There are a number of methods you can use to identify the decision-makers in your target business.

Use the Internet - customers often give biographies and contact details for key members of staff on their websites. If you don't know their website address, try entering the business name in a search engine.

Telephone the business to ask who's responsible for purchasing your particular product or service.

Keep an eye on the trade press - articles on potential customers will often include a quote from a senior manager.

Get hold of marketing literature - it can be a fruitful source of useful contact information.

Attend trade fairs and exhibitions and chat to staff on the stands of your target customers. If you're lucky you may meet a decision-maker - and even if you don't the people there should be able to point you in the right direction.

Once you're armed with information on the key decision-makers, it's time to make that **first crucial contact** with them.

First consider what the particular customer is worth to you - this will help you decide how much time to invest in selling to them.

Many businesses find that potential customers are more receptive in the morning. To some extent, however, it's a matter of trial and error. You may find, for instance, that Monday mornings are a bad time to call because people are busy organising themselves for the week ahead.

Often personal assistants and other employees may be asked to shield their managers from unwanted sales calls. So you'll need to convince them to put you through to the decision-maker.

This will involve:
- Showing some knowledge of their business

- Explaining briefly how the decision-maker would benefit from taking your call
- Being persistent and dealing with brush-offs

Getting a meeting

The main purpose of many sales calls is to get an appointment with a potential customer. Once you get through to the person you're targeting, you need to persuade them why it's worth meeting you.

It's a good idea to plan what you're going to say in advance. You may have as little as 10 to 20 seconds to get the customer's attention before they lose interest - so you've got to say something that will make them listen. Be ready for common brush-offs.

Pick one key benefit of your product or service and tailor the way you present it to fit the particular customer's needs.

If the customer sounds interested in what you've got to offer, ask for a meeting to discuss things further. Propose a time that's convenient for you and let the customer come back with an alternative if they wish. Always offer to visit customers at their own premises - they will be less likely to cancel the appointment.

Deal with common brush-offs

Getting the brush-off is a fact of life for any sales person. The key to success is learning the most common brush-offs and planning in advance how you will handle them.

Always aim to keep developing the relationship with the customer. The longer you can keep the conversation going, the more chance you have of getting them interested. Here are some examples of common brush-offs and how you might deal with them.

You hear: "Put something in the post to me/send me an email."

You reply: "No problem. What is it that you're particularly interested in?" "OK. I'll send you some basic information and then I can call you next week to discuss it."

You hear: "I'll need to think about it."
You reply: "Of course. What are your particular concerns?"

You hear: "I'm afraid I haven't got time to speak now."
You reply: "That's fine. I'll send you an email following up on our discussion."
"OK. When would be a good time to talk instead?"

Sometimes you will get an outright brush-off - the customer will make it clear they are not interested at all. If this happens, try to find out why. It may be that a follow-up call in a few months' time may be better received. And don't let a refusal get you down - the next customer you speak with may sense the disappointment in your voice.

Sell the benefits, not the features

Customers don't just want to know how your product or service works - they want to know what benefits it will bring them

So sell the benefits, not the features. Businesses and consumers don't buy on price alone. Your customers want to know what your product or service can do for them, not just how it works.

They want value for money and that could include paying more for the benefits or advantages they gain from buying your product or service.

The key to selling the benefits of your product or service is to look at them through the eyes of the person you are selling to. The more you know about your customers' needs, the easier this will be.

Step back

You may be fascinated by the specifications of the washing machines you sell and their components. But the benefits you'd want to emphasise to the customer are low noise and the ability to produce spotless clothes a low temperature, therefore helping the customer to be friendly to the environment.

Match the needs of the individual customer to what your product or service can offer. For example: if you're running a next-day stationery supplies service for other businesses, what you are really selling are the benefits of, namely:

Uninterrupted workflow
General business efficiency
Staff who aren't frustrated when the paper runs out
Office space not taken up by piles of paper, staples and toner
Value for money, they spend when they need it

Softer issues

You may need to look at softer, more emotional issues when identifying the benefits of a personal consumer product. For example, a mobile phone may have Internet access, but unless it looks cool it's dead in the teenage market.

And some businesses may incorporate softer issues into hard-nosed buying decisions. For example, if you're running a media design and buying agency you may pay over the odds for flashy PC screens and stylish furniture because you want clients to know you have high design values.

Matching benefits to the customers' needs

You need to match benefits to a customer's needs when you're:

> Having conversations with customers
> Preparing a sales proposal
> Making a sales presentation
> Researching sales literature for a target audience

Find out what the customer wants and don't try to bend their wishes to suit your product or service. Ask questions to find out what they're hoping to achieve from the purchase. Encourage them to ask lots of questions, too.

Ask more general questions about the customer you're dealing with, don't just talk about their needs in relation to their use of your product or service. The answers may give you clues to unexpected benefits.

Do homework beforehand on the customer and their marketplace so you can ask informed questions and make them confident you have some understanding of their needs.

Use this information to analyse your product and identify what factors are most likely to make the customer buy.

It helps if you can quantify any benefits in money or time terms, especially where the advantages of a particular product or service outweigh the costs. Let your customer know if buying your product now will help them make cost savings or boost their own turnover.

And remember that businesses in particular can feel more confident about buying if you can show how other businesses have benefited from what you're selling.

Sales methods

These are the basic rules of selling. They are always the same, whether you're dealing with customers in person, by phone or whether it's in a business-to-business or retail environment.

There are four basic steps to making a sale, these are:

- Get the customer's **A**ttention
- Stimulate the customer's **I**nterest
- Create the **D**esire to buy
- Confirm the **A**ction to be taken

This is often referred to as AIDA

To stop a potential customer switching off or putting the phone down straight away, take the following precautions:

- Do some research beforehand
- Prevent your brochure from going straight in the bin or the listener from turning off by gaining their attention with an eye-catching design or thought-provoking statement
- Explain the benefits of purchasing. Don't just talk about the efficiency of a floor cleaner. Say that it will also reduce staff costs and the customer's maintenance bill. Explaining the benefits creates the desire to buy

- A call to action - such as a time-limited offer - can also help prompt a customer to buy, or at least find out more
- A golden rule is to always include your telephone number, address, email address or order form on all literature.

At the end of a sales conversation repeat what has been agreed and the next steps, such as delivery times. Send a confirmatory email or letter.

Talk to your customers and LISTEN

When you speak to any customer, your primary aim should be to find out as much about their needs as possible. Knowing what they want to do or achieve will help build a picture of what you can do for them - and open new opportunities for sales.

It's worth taking notes of each conversation and referring to them before you call or visit. This can help build a relationship. For example, if a contact mentions an upcoming holiday, you can ask if they enjoyed themselves next time you speak.

Learn to **listen** - often the best sales people are those who listen more than they talk. Being attentive to the customer's needs makes them feel important. You may also pick up on information to help make a sale.

Ask the right questions - always start with questions that can only be answered "Yes". For example, asking your contact if they would like to increase efficiency or quality is unlikely to get a negative response.

Move on to open-ended questions that will reveal more about their needs. A pensions salesperson might ask when a customer plans to review their financial arrangements.

To help gauge interest, ask the customer if they have any questions about your product or service. If they ask questions such as "When can you deliver?" or "How many do you have in stock?" take it as a cue to close the sale.

You want to learn to sell effectively

Making successful sales presentations

There are some simple tips for you to remember when making a sales presentation

Start by working out the key message you want the audience to remember. Always focus on the needs of the customer. For example, if you're talking to a managing director about a new software package, you might stress how it will save time. When speaking to employees, you might emphasise how it would make their jobs easier.

Most people recall most clearly what is said at the beginning and end, so build your key points into these sections.

Organise what you want to say into sections, building up a logical case to buy your goods or services.

Think about any objections or points the audience might raise and make the responses part of the presentation.

Find facts and figures that support your argument, such as businesses that have already benefited from your product or service.

Make sure you know the products and services of your competitors as well as your own and be ready to answer questions.

Avoid having to ask anyone to hold or wait for you to find out something, most will not take kindly to being told to be silent. A really confident speaker can take questions off the cuff and come across as completely customer-focused.

Summing up for action

Distribute handouts only at the end of the presentation so your audience stays focused on you while you're speaking. Handouts can summarise what you've said but can include additional material, case studies, product samples, marketing literature and contact details.

If you're using presentation technology such as PowerPoint, make sure you've got handouts of all the screens. You will also need them if something goes wrong.

When you've dealt with any queries, establish the next steps, such as asking if they want to order or arrange another meeting.

Using presentation technology

If you are presenting at your own premises, set everything up in advance. When visiting elsewhere confirm your technical requirements beforehand.

Turn projectors and other equipment off when not needed so as to avoid distracting attention from what you are saying.

Always make sure you have hard-copy printouts in case the technology lets you down.

Use caution

There are some common mistakes you can avoid by heeding the following advice:

- Go easy on technology - it increases the chances of something going wrong
- Don't put basic information on a screen - it can come across as patronising
- Don't allow your physical presentation aids to dominate the proceedings - your audience wants to see and hear you
- Let somebody else operate the machine - your audience want you to talk to them, not to a screen or a machine

Handling objections

Before visiting, calling or making a presentation, try to identify any reasons a customer might give not to purchase.

You want to learn to sell effectively

Some of your predictions will be based on knowledge of the marketplace, the competition and previous conversations with your customer.

Think about possible responses and remember that not all objections are negative. Sometimes they show the customer is interested.

The positive response

Summarise what you believe the objections are and try to answer each one in turn.

Ask the customer to clarify what they mean if you're unsure. If they say a product or service is too expensive, they may mean it's above budget and they aren't interested. But they may mean they would buy with a discount.

Test each objection to see if there is anything you can do about it until the sale is dependent on the last objection.

Start talking about taking an order. If they are reluctant because of your delivery schedule, ask if they will place the order if you bring the delivery forward.

The most common objection is likely to be price. Think beforehand about how you can counter it. Will buying save them more money than they spend or can you offer flexible payment terms? Stress all-round value for money and gains in efficiency or time.

Accepting no for an answer

You won't always be able to meet all objections. Let the customer know you'll always be available to answer any other queries and, if they seem at all interested, keep in touch. Their circumstances or yours may change, allowing you to make a sale at a later stage.

Negotiating a sale

Both you and the customer want to get the best possible deal. Here are some guidelines for you to consider once you have caught the attention of the customer and there is a prospect of a sale

DO:

Try to understand the customer's needs. Use questions to find out as much as you can about their alternatives and budget

Decide how important the deal is. Could it bring in more business or significantly boost your cash flow?

Set out your objectives and decide which are negotiable - but don't disclose these thoughts

Consider price, volume and timing and whether you will give a reduction on a larger quantity or for paying cash straight away

Listen carefully to what the customer is saying

Ask for a break if you need time to think

Summarise the decisions you have reached

Shake on it - no one likes to back out of a deal

DON'T:

Appear too keen. If it's too obvious you need the deal, the price may get pushed down

Give any indication at the start that you might be willing to concede

You want to learn to sell effectively

Name a starting price or say you will accept a near offer

Make concessions too easily

Give unnecessary discounts. Other customers may find out and become resentful

Make last-minute concessions. If someone has agreed to buy, don't throw in extras free.

Dealing with sales nerves
Making a presentation or a sales call - face-to-face or on the phone - can be a big challenge. But preparation and practice can go a long way. It is normal to have a degree of nerves and it can even be useful to keep you on your toes. Someone who is over-confident is more likely to get carried away and may even come across as insincere. To ensure you stay in control:

- Always be well prepared
- Rehearse what you're going to say a few times - ideally to an audience of family, friends or colleagues
- Try to speak slowly. Keep a glass of water close by and take a few deep breaths before starting to speak
- When making an important phone call, standing up can help you feel more confident and in control. Smiling will also make you feel - and sound - more positive
- If giving a presentation, practise in the room where you'll be speaking or try to visualise yourself giving the speech
- If you think you're likely to shake, avoid holding pieces of paper that will display your nerves to the audience.

You want to get retailers to take your product

Study the sales techniques used by supermarkets to get customers to stay inside and spend more. These include:

- Layout - putting items such as sweets near the till or placing common products at different ends of a shop can encourage impulse purchases
- In-store promotions - banners and captions around the shop pushing special offers and new products
- Loss leaders - these heavily discounted items are often found next to more expensive ones. (If customers think they're getting a good deal on one product, they're more likely to splash out on another)
- Three for the price of two - useful if margins and total revenue justify it or if you use the offer as a loss leader
- Pricing products at odd value - selling something at €24.95 rather than €25, for example, is a common tactic.

If you sell through somebody else's shop you need to think about how you can persuade the retailers to stock your products - and display them prominently.

It's worth carrying out research to identify the needs of a particular shop and its target market. You're then in a better position to tell the retailer how they will benefit from stocking your product and how your product differs from what they already offer.

Retailers will want to know how you plan to market your product, as well as being interested in how well your product sells. Other concerns may include how the product complements an existing range and how quickly you can provide more stock on demand.

You want to learn how to close a sale

I love going for the close! Here are the basic techniques for getting a customer to commit to a purchase

You close a sale when you get a customer to commit to purchasing your product or service.

Remember your commitment to the customer doesn't stop once you've closed a deal. Good after-sales care will make customers more likely to return.

It's a good idea to tread carefully. Going for the hard sell and putting pressure on customers to buy may boost your sales, but you risk making them feel unhappy with their purchase. This could make customers less likely to buy from you again.

They may even return the goods or cancel a service agreement when they've had time to think things over more carefully.

You should try to establish a continuing relationship with all your customers. This is particularly important for customers who might want to return for repeat orders.

How to close with existing customers

The usual techniques for closing sales are not always appropriate for customers with whom you have a continuing dialogue and buying relationship.

Your customer relationship management (CRM) policy will dictate when to nudge an existing customer into raising an invoice for a repeat order.

It will also determine how you talk to the customer about their continuing needs and when you might upsell them to higher-value or newer products.

Your customer will expect you to ask about timescales and whether a decision is likely. You could say it would be helpful to know so you can plan the necessary work and make sure a valued customer is not at the back of the queue.

Simple techniques to close a sale

Although there are numerous techniques to close a sale, you don't necessarily need to use all of them. In certain circumstances some or even all of them may not be useful - with an existing loyal customer, for instance.

Use your judgement about the personality of the person you're dealing with - how will they react?

Create a sense of urgency if things are really dragging. You need to convince the customer they need your product - now. Let them know that if they don't purchase straight away, they could miss a good deal. Tell them if an offer is about to end or if booking early will get them a better price.

Listen for buying signals from the customer such as:

Have you got many left?
How soon could you deliver?
Have you got it in blue?

Once you hear a buying signal, **stop selling**. Otherwise you risk talking yourself out of the sale.

Don't be afraid to **ask for the sale**. You could simply say "Can I take your order now?" Try to sound positive and upbeat.

Giving the customer alternatives can be an effective way to close a sale. So a furniture sales person could ask: "Do you want the bookcase in oak or mahogany?"

If the customer has one remaining objection, you can often win them over by making a solution to this problem a condition of the sale. So you might say: "If I guarantee to move the delivery date forward, will you place your order now?"

After all objections have been met, **stop talking** and allow the customer time to make a decision.

If they say yes, confirm the deal. Make sure the customer is happy with what has been agreed and follow this up later in writing or with a telephone call.

If they still say no, accept their decision. Let them know you will be happy to help if they need further information.

You want to submit a bid for a contract

Knowing how to prepare bids and tenders can help you win private- and public sector business. This includes understanding how to identify potential contracts, what to include in your tender and how to write it for the best chance of success.

Submitting a bid is common for businesses supplying goods or services to other businesses or the public sector. At a basic level you expect to quote for a job or write a letter saying why you should be given the business.

But more formal tenders often apply to bigger jobs or for supply contracts spread over time. You'll find public-sector work in particular has specific tendering processes. This applies to customers ranging from your local authority or hospital to a government department.

Even if you don't win the work this time, writing a tender can clarify your aims, strengths and weaknesses and you can learn for next time by asking for feedback on your bid. It raises your profile with the customer and helps you learn about customers' needs.

Should you bid?
Preparing tenders can help you to win big orders, but it can also be time-consuming, cost money and tie up valuable resources. If you don't get the contract the money and time spent is usually lost, so you need to weigh up whether a tender is worth bidding for. Key actions to take and points to consider are:

1. Get hold of the bid documents and analyse them
2. Make sure you can match the technical, skill and experience requirements
3. How much will it cost to prepare your bid?

4. Would the work fit in with your strategy and positioning of your business?
5. Estimate the costs of fulfilling the contract and whether you'd make enough money
6. Assess how the contract would affect your other work, staffing and ability to take on other new business
7. You also need to consider how important the customer is to your business. Is this a good potential client or one you don't want to offend by not tendering? Try to understand things from the client's point of view.

Find out what the client wants
Many potential clients will talk things through on an informal basis before you decide to bid. Seek a meeting or telephone discussion. You should always raise questions by phone or email if tender documents are unclear - on anything from deadlines to how you'd get paid.

Make sure the client is **serious**; you're not there to make up the numbers or to test the market. Sometimes customers may just be fishing for ideas they'll then use for themselves. But don't forget many clients genuinely want you to make a creative contribution and provide ideas.

What to put in your tender
Once you've decided to bid, you'll need to decide how you'll manage the bid:

1. Who gathers information and does research?
2. Who co-ordinates all the material you need?
3. Who writes the drafts?
4. Who checks them?
5. How will the rest of your firm's work get done?

Crucial rules for your tender document

1. Focus on the client - talk about their needs and how you can solve their problems. When you speak about yourself, it's to prove you have the skills, experience and organisation to fulfil the client's requirements.
2. Help the client by coming up with ideas - from alternative ways of doing things to how to tackle possible worries about future maintenance and staffing implications.
3. Value for money, and not price alone, decides most bids. It means bringing something to the work that can't be done by the client. Emphasise business benefits, service improvements, risk reduction, low maintenance, quality, reliability, previous satisfied customers, lifetime costs etc.
4. Analyse all of the cost and pricing factors of the contract. Don't ignore fixed costs such as wages for staff members who could be working on something else.
5. Contract management - show you have the resources to do the work and a feasible, cost-effective way to meet the client's needs, hit deadlines and respond flexibly to changing situations.
6. Show you've thought about - and can manage - potential financial, commercial and legal risks that could cause contract failure.
7. Give details of your team. Emphasise strengths. CVs should highlight successes with similar projects as well as qualifications and experience.

Writing your tender

Make sure you **match the bid specification** and answer all questions. Summarise your bid and why it answers the client's needs. Write this last but put it at the beginning of your tender.

You want to learn to sell effectively

Clients will also expect you to:

- State the purpose and origin of the bid
- Summarise your work as a contractor, past experience and credentials for this job
- Say how you'll carry out the work and how and when the client's aims will be achieved
- Explain the benefits and value-for-money of your bid
- Detail when and how goods and services are to be delivered and provide a timetable
- Demonstrate your team's skills, experience of similar work and their responsibilities if you win the contract
- Explain how you will manage the project
- Give details of your pricing and any aftercare arrangements within the price
- Be practical and identify potential problems without promising what's clearly impossible for you to deliver

Include a covering letter that responds to the bid invitation, summarises your main message and explains how the documents are organised.

Tips on how to present your tender

It is well worth spending some time on your tender, paying attention to the presentation, for example:

1. Keep sentences and paragraphs short, punchy and businesslike

2. Use bullet points and headings to break up text

3. Decide on a typeface, layout and type size - not too small - and stick to them

4. Make sure everything is standardised - are CVs all presented in the same way?

5. Be careful when cut-and-pasting copy to make sure the format stays the same

6. Make sure you've developed a logical argument and everything hangs together

7. Read everything again. Then get a colleague to read it - for meaning, typing mistakes and omissions

8. Use appendices for supporting additional information

9. On the front cover state the project title, date, who the tender has been prepared for and your company details

10. Include a contents page

11. Number paragraphs so material can be located

12. Consider getting it bound professionally (don't get job applications bound though)

Make it simple

Make it memorable

Make it inviting to look at

Make it a pleasure to read

Ask for the sale!

Meet the Bullies

The most recent large-scale study of workplace experiences found that as many as one in ten people were bullied at work within the previous six months alone. The figure rises to one in four within the last five years.

Bullying has existed since the industrial revolution. But there's definitely an increasing ability to talk about it. So what should you do if you think you're being bullied?

Identifying the species of your bully can help you deal with him or her without having to resort to the law. There are **broadly two types of bully**. First there is the kind of individual who likes to be **in control**. They tend to be well aware of the effects of their behaviour. They use this to manipulate people.

These power mongers generally have to be dealt with at a structural level, using organisational procedures to put boundaries on their behaviour and curb the aggression that wasn't properly managed in childhood. In extreme cases this kind of bullying tips into actual psychopathy. There is a small group of psychopaths in management who simply shouldn't be there. They are untrainable.

The **second broad category** of bully is the **perfectionist** who can become very intolerant of mistakes, including their own. They often don't realise they are bullying, and once they find out they tend to be very willing to engage in the development process to sort it out.

Within these two broad categories there are several types of bully. It is possible to deal with many of these and not all instances of bullying have to end in high profile court cases and emotionally destroyed targets. If you are not being bullied, then you have nothing to worry about, although be careful not to collude inadvertently with bullies by ganging up on and excluding the bully's targets! The key is to identify what motivates your bully and learn how to handle them. **Sometimes that means staying well out of the bully's way.**

People **become bullies** through three different routes: personality, by reading cues in political workplaces and by accident.

What is discrimination?

The Employment Equality Act, 1998 outlaws discriminatory practices in relation to and within employment. The Act prohibits direct and indirect discrimination and victimisation in employment on **nine grounds**. These are: gender; marital status; family status; sexual orientation; religion; age; disability; race; membership of the Traveller Community. All aspects of employment are covered: equal pay; access to employment; vocational training; conditions of employment; work experience; promotion and dismissal.

What is harassment?

The Employment Equality Act 1998, defines sexual harassment as unwanted physical intimacy, requests for sexual favours, spoken words and gestures and the display or circulation of written words, pictures or other materials in the workplace. Unwelcome requests or conduct that could reasonably be regarded as sexual or otherwise on the gender ground, offensive, humiliating or intimidating, will constitute sexual harassment. Harassment on the **nine grounds** listed above is unlawful.

What is bullying?

Persistent offensive, abusive, intimidating, malicious or insulting behaviour. Abuse of power. Carried out directly or indirectly. May be carried out by an individual or group. A once-off incident may amount to misconduct, but not bullying. However, it may be that the same individual has meted out the same treatment to several people, in which case there is a pattern and a case of bullying can be made.

Do you recognise any of these people?

Meet Seething Sean, a chronic bully

A lifetime of bullying behind him

Motto: attack, deny, counterattack, retaliate!

Seething Sean is a **chronic bully**. Wherever you encounter Seething Sean, he will try to dominate you. He bullies checkout staff in supermarkets as well as colleagues and subordinates in his workplace. He has no intention of changing. "You don't like it? Then LEAVE" is a regular scream.

Seething Sean is an inadequate, poorly developed person. Incapable of confronting his own feelings of inadequacy, and without the self-control to accept and address his own flaws, deep down he loathes himself.

You'll hear Seething Sean berating even his own parents. He makes comments such as "I can't stand to be with them for more than half an hour".

He deflects this self-loathing by inventing flaws in others, flaws that reflect his own shortcomings, and launches regular irrational attacks on them. He then feels great!

Seething Sean's narcissistic personality has been groomed over his entire lifetime. He is well used to getting his way in every situation. Nobody stands up to him. They simply turn away, in fear or indifference. Except for other bullies, who suck up to him and are well rewarded.

Seething Sean is both disliked and feared by those who work for him. He is mean and nasty at work. He inflicts harm on some colleagues and manipulates all of them in some way. He destroys careers and inflicts emotional turmoil on his targets. For Seething Sean, there is simply no substitute for the thrill of humbling other people into subservience. Cruelty is such bliss; he can't conceal his delighted grin when he scores a public victory.

He is a sadist and a sociopath. He is one of the few types of bully that cannot be treated or changed.

This doesn't hold Sean back. Though chronic bullies are fairly rare, his competitive workplace has several specimens. Like him, they are considered great leaders and more and more power is heaped on them. This is what his CV would look like.

****

Seething Sean's CV

Profession: Chronic Bully

Motto: attack, deny, counterattack, retaliate!

Summary: mean, cunning, conniving, scheming, calculating, cruel, sadistic, ruthless, treacherous, premeditated, exploitative, pernicious, malevolent, obnoxious, opportunist, unconcerned – and *proud* of it.

Objective: I'm here to inflict pain on others. I must be the centre of attention. I crave power, control, domination and subjugation.

Interpersonal Skills
None. I conceal this by relying on rules, procedures, aggression, denial and mimicry. Pretty good at faking. Excel at passing aggression off as assertiveness.

Meet the bullies

Achievements
I end careers and leave my targets in emotional shreds

Have a hang up about bodily functions; one of proudest achievements was filling the ladies toilets with filing cabinets, parking my desk in front of the door and complaining 'everyone has to pass me to go to the loo'. All those whining women had to share a 2-stall loo with all the men in the building. (A true and current example in the Dublin headquarters of a financially highly successful, multi-national, indigenous Irish company).

Skills
My species shows some variety here. I will either:
- Be incompetent and bully to disguise this
- Be good at carrying out rule-based or procedurally-oriented jobs which require no free thinking or imagination but am guaranteed to fail if required to step outside this role, eg dealing with people
- Excel in one area of work (prefer science or numbers), may be regarded as the leading authority in my field, lack interpersonal skills; enjoy physical aggression and sexual harassment.

Abilities
Relish holding power over people. This is a synch; it's *so* easy to take people in.

My bullying strategies for this are:
Disempower the target so they depend on me. They'd better; otherwise I'll make every day a living hell.

Charm an emotionally needy colleague into supporting me; often this person will become my advocate. Such people are bullies-in-training. My favourite behaves like an angry hippo when I'm not around, and beams like a besotted Miss Piggy on sight of Kermit as soon as I appear (well, I *am* a joy to behold, I must say!)

Cover my tracks with my easy charm with superiors – they never catch sight of my constant lying!

Never accept responsibility: deny, counterattack, retaliate and, if need be, pretend to be the victim. Have a couple of answers ready such as "this is so minor it's not worth talking about..." and the new start line "I can't think why you're so keen to focus on the past" and "what's past is past, I'll forget your behaviour and we'll start afresh". (This is a tactic for the bully to absolve himself of all responsibility while at the same time using fake conciliation to divert attention.)

Excel at retaliation and counterattack. Follow denial with an aggressive counter-attack of counter-criticism or counter-allegation, often based on distortion or fabrication. Lying, deception, duplicity, hypocrisy and blame are key. My purpose is to avoid answering the question and so avoid accepting responsibility. With luck, my wimpy target can be tricked into giving another long, boring account to prove me wrong; by the time they have finished droning on, everybody will have forgotten the original question.

Strategy when backed into a corner
When wimpy target looks like proving me wrong (seldom happens, denial and counterattack usually work a dream) pretend to be the victim. If this seems implausible, burst into tears (people *hate* that and won't know what to do!) or pretend to be deeply offended. Have been known to portray the target as the bad guy and/ or to present false claims. Works a dream on new hires.

Other tactics include manipulating people's perceptions to portray themselves as the injured party and the target as the villain of the piece. Or presenting as a false victim.

(Note to aspiring bullies: sometimes a talented bully will suddenly claim to be suffering "stress" and go off on long-term sick leave, although no one can quite establish why. Alleged ill-health can also be a useful vehicle for gaining attention and sympathy.)

Career Masterstroke
Excel at using anger to control my targets.
Targets, who may have taken months to reach this stage, see me (their tormentor!) getting away with it and can easily be provoked into an angry and emotional outburst. Yes! All I have to do is say "I told you so". My target becomes the bad guy. Clever or what!

Publications
Wrote *The Bully's 10 Commandments*. See these on following page.

****

The Bully's 10 Commandments

A work of literary genius penned by a gifted chronic bully

1. Criticise and question the ability of your targets

2. Blame your target for errors (ideally ones you have contrived!)

3. Make unreasonable work demands

4. Be consistently inconsistent when it comes to rules

5. Use the threat of job loss at every opportunity

6. Insult, put-down, destroy

7. Dismiss and deny target's achievements

8. Yell, scream, gesticulate wildly

9. Steal credit for target's work

10. Exclude, freeze-out, isolate

Signed: ***Seething Sean, Chronic Bully***

****

A complete prat, isn't he?

Aha, cue to bully

Meet Mouthy Mandy, opportunist bully

Says: please stand still while I trample on you

Mouthy Mandy features in plenty of workplaces. She is an expert at reading political cues at work. And when the opportunity strikes, she bullies.

Mouthy Mandy is an **opportunist bully**. Very skilled in phoney smiles and little laughs, she is comfortable in very competitive environments, where you win by trampling all over other people.

She'd be appalled to be called a bully. In her mind, she is simply climbing (over you) to the top. It's nothing personal, simply business. She's a survivor and has already convinced her supporters that she can do no wrong.

Mouthy Mandy will continue to connive and bully for as long as she is allowed. She is acting in a way that her environment accepts. She would stop in a flash if she faced any punishment for her behaviour.

Interestingly, Mouthy Mandy is not a chronic bully; she is in fact an excellent parent, neighbour and citizen.

This kind of bully can be dealt with. If you find yourself managing this bully, the best way to address the problem is to change the environment, ie make bullying unacceptable.

A simply rule in countering bullying is to impose a '*back-it-up-or-shut-up*' rule. Make the bullies substantiate their claims or withdraw them. This is a very effective policy, as bullies often reply on manipulating the emotions of senior people.

Whoops, did I bully you

Meet Jovial John, benign bully

Likely to say: just hurry up!

Jovial John is a senior executive in a media company. He is a superb salesperson. He doesn't hesitate to call on experts to help. Jovial John's problem is that he has very little patience. He'll start to demonstrate something new, lose patience and do it himself. He will devote unlimited time to making a sale (nothing wrong with that, he always make the sale).

For example, the benign bully will follow to the letter what the company's Human Resource manager advises in difficult situations.

But, hey, that looked so easy! Guys, never mind this HR stuff, *just do it your own way*.

Next time, he goes solo with union negotiations and ends up stuck, while his 'empowered' team plunge the company into a series of lawsuits because they failed to follow fair procedure in some minor disciplinary matters and got carried away with the battle cry "you're fired!"

Jovial John is not a particularly harmful type of bully. Once confronted with his bullying, he will usually be shocked and apologise. He is likely to be concerned at the implications his behaviour will have for the organisation. He probably will not repeat the bullying.

Turn off that whining PLEASE!

Meet Harold, professional nag

Likely to say: don't you wanna be me?

Senior management adores Harold. He gets results from his people! By constantly criticising and putting them down.

Harold is a **negative perfectionist, a constant critic, and a professional nag**. He could take Olympic Gold in whining, complaining and finding fault. He wouldn't give a toss about being caught bending the rules, he'll always have someone else to blame.

Deeply personally insecure, Harold is one tough guy to the outside world. Not unlike cults that take ownership of members' whole mind and person, this kind of bully will encourage you to doubt your abilities while he demolishes your self-confidence. His tactics will include:

- Aggressive body-language, waving his arms, glaring at you while he speaks (or shouts)
- Insults, derogatory comments, put-downs
- Constant complaints and innuendo about your incompetence
- Unreasonable demands for work, unachievable deadlines
- Fabricates errors and blames you for them
- Adjusts records to make you look bad (eg you are required to clock-in for work, are on-time but the bully amends the record to change the time)
- Launches a constant blitz of emails that require responses, adding to your workload
- Traps the targets by insisting that complaints go with the chain of command, starting with him.

Venom alert!

Here comes the Friendly Viper

Appearance: phoney smile

Most likely to say: '*would you like to have lunch?*' so that she can collect information to sabotage you and '*I had no idea things had got to this stage, hope things work out well for you in the future*' (just not here!) after she has helped to engineer your downfall.

The friendly viper will pretend to be your friend while she sabotages you. Her friendliness is simply a means of gleaning information from you to be used later against you. Her phoney smile disguises her naked aggression. She will shred your reputation with more senior people and will make herself the favourite of people with power. The friendly viper bullies by controlling how other people perceive her target. She lies habitually, is skilled at feigning loyalty to senior people and is really obsessed only with herself. Tactics employed by the friendly viper will include:

- Denying her target access to the resources required to do his or her job (key to the office, paper for the printer, delays passing on memos with information on deadlines)
- Divides and conquers; elicits negative information from colleagues, who will be made to suffer it they don't cooperate
- Is rude, patronising and condescending to the target, while maintaining 'butter-wouldn't-melt-in-my-mouth' image in front of others

Meet the bullies

- Gossips about the target with colleagues
- Overuses sexuality to score points

The friendly viper is literally bursting with conceit and sincerely believes she is an expert in areas where she has either no talent or only a very small amount of knowledge. She is particularly convinced she is technically talented, though the opposite if often true. She is the type who will watch a couple of episodes of *ER* or *Casualty* and then push a qualified nurse out of the way at an accident scene so that she, *the real expert*, can assist the injured victim.

If she hasn't already schemed her way into such a role, the friendly viper will be desperate *to manage*. Often in areas in which she has no expertise. According to the friendly viper, managing is just about giving orders to people.

Often, the friendly viper is also a bit thick. In an odd way, that's part of her power. The target feels as though he or she is complaining about someone less capable – mocking the afflicted - so often remains silent.

However, if you are on the receiving end of a dose of the friendly viper's venom, keep an eye on the mess she is likely to be making of her, er, 'managing'. There is a good chance she will leave a trail of evidence showing how inept she really is, especially if she has spoofed her way into something like finance or IT; it is your choice how and when to produce the evidence. Sometimes the smart move is to wait for some time, until the friendly viper has had a really good opportunity to show how fabulous, or utterly useless, she is at her job.

So the smartest move if faced with the friendly viper often is: *smile back at her*, give her only the information that suits you and then start collecting evidence of her ineffective work, to be used at your convenience in a counteroffensive.

The bully is having an affair with another member of staff

What a surprise. Is the bully a friendly viper by any chance?

The affair has little to do with friendship, and a lot to do with strategic alliance in pursuit of power, control, domination and subjugation. Sometimes, the relationship with another member of staff is based not so much on sexual attraction but on a mutual admiration for the way in which each other behaves.

If the **bully is a female** in a junior position, she finds a weak male in a senior position (this is usually not difficult) - for example the managing director, any senior executive, finance director, HR director, or any other departmental director – and then gains patronage, protection and reward (eg promotion) by 'traditional' methods.

Once promotion is gained, the female calculates who can give her the next promotion; if the first male cannot deliver, he is ditched and another adopted. The males are unlikely to admit this is happening or has happened. Understandably. They look like fools and, though this is very apparent to almost everyone, they kind of hope nobody has noticed.

If the **bully is a male** in a senior position, he is often sleeping with a secretary or office administrator, as this is where he gets his information and where he spreads his disinformation. If there is no physical affair, he will ensure she believes she is in love with him. Sometimes the female junior can be identified by her reward, eg being the only person allowed to hold the keys of the stock cupboard (everyone has to grovel to her if they want a new pen), or being put in charge of the office in the bully's absence when there are others who are senior to her who would make more appropriate deputies. She will also get away with, and perhaps even rewarded for, misconduct if it benefits the bully. By helping scupper the career of the bully's peer, for example.

140

What does bullying do to your health?

Bullying causes injury to health and makes you ill. How many of these symptoms do you have?

- Constant high levels of stress and anxiety
- Frequent illness such as viral infections especially flu and glandular fever, colds, coughs, chest, ear, nose and throat infections (stress plays havoc with your immune system)
- Aches and pains in the joints and muscles with no obvious cause; also back pain with no obvious cause and which won't go away or respond to treatment
- Headaches and migraines
- Tiredness, exhaustion, constant fatigue
- Sleeplessness, nightmares, waking early, waking up more tired than when you went to bed
- Flashbacks and replays, obsessive thoughts, can't get the bullying out of your mind
- Skin problems such as eczema, psoriasis, athlete's foot, ulcers, shingles
- Poor concentration, can't concentrate on anything for long
- Bad or intermittently-functioning memory, forgetfulness, especially with trivial day-to-day things
- Sweating, trembling, shaking, palpitations, panic attacks
- Bursting into tears regularly and over trivial matters
- Uncharacteristic irritability and angry outbursts
- Hyper vigilance, being constantly on edge
- Hypersensitivity, fragility, isolation, withdrawal
- Reactive depression, lethargy, hopelessness, anger
- Shattered self-confidence, low self-esteem

That's what bullying can do to the target's health. Sometimes the bully suffers too – massive stress, heart condition, and obesity.

Dealing with bullies

Why do people say things like 'you'll get over it eventually' (you will in most cases, but may have lost a couple of years of your life to stress and worry in the meantime), 'just ignore them' (yeah!), 'and don't worry about it'. Such advice is well intentioned, you *know* that, but it doesn't usually help very much.

But what if you were able to do just that? To simply not allow other people's misconduct to bother you?

What do I mean by that? Soldiering on, suffering in silence, keeping a stiff upper lip? Absolutely not! This will only prolong your agony.

If you are in stress now, then decide whom you can trust to talk to about your situation. Let them know you need their help, and also their confidence. You don't want your difficulties to be broadcast all over the place; equally, when this is all behind you, you want to be able to talk to that person in the future about unrelated matters, secure in the knowledge that they too have put your difficulties behind them, and will not raise the matter again unless you do so first.

Because confidentiality, and at times complete detachment, is important, your confidant may not actually be your best friend, spouse or partner at all, but someone more neutral. It may be someone you never see again.

So, deciding to talk about the bullying is an important step to take.

On a longer-term basis, I strongly recommend that you learn a habit that will immunise you from being bothered too much by other people's misconduct in the future.

The way to do this is to learn to detach you from certain situations. Don't panic employers! I am not recommending that your employees stop being committed. Sometimes one of the reasons why a target of bullying becomes so upset by the treatment they receive is that he or she is *too* emotionally attached to their job/ employer. He feels as though family has betrayed him.

The first step in converting the pain you experience when you're bullied – feelings of hurt, anger, dismay, hopelessness - is to take control of this emotional turbulence. Reacting angrily really doesn't help. Equally, smothering your anger so that it smoulders away, only to erupt at some later point, is not helpful either. Why fuel painful, destructive emotions when you can covert them into positive emotions? Before you can take responsibility for the emotion you must recognise it. What are you feeling? Where in your body do you feel this emotion? Your natural instinct will be to avoid the pain; it will damage you much less if you deal with it as it occurs, rather than burying it to explode at some later date.

You'll find exercises to help you convert negative and angry reactions into a positive emotion about your life starting on page 201. Get in the habit of practising these exercises. That way, when you face a bully or some other difficult situation at work, you will be able to maintain control and *respond* calmly, instead of *reacting* in a way that you regret later.

You may want to take a moment to practice the calming exercise now. You'll find it on page 206.

Ready to deal with the bullies then?

The first thing to remember is that until such time as they are treated or removed, the bully will not stop his or her bullying behaviour. They are incapable of behaving in any other way. Pathetic, isn't it?

You, on the other hand, are a normal human being, intelligent, accomplished, well liked, you have a life, and often you are happy, except when you're on the receiving end of the bully's terrorist tactics.

The point is that, no matter how rough things get, *you* have control over the amount of hurt this thug can inflict on you. Let me stress first that you should never dismiss the option of complaining about bullying and other misconduct. What I am talking about here is not public justice, it is about limiting, and when you get the hang of it, completing excluding the damage the bully can inflict on you. So keep practicing staying positive.

When called to account for the way they have chosen to behave, mature adults do not respond by bursting into tears. If you're dealing with a serial bully who has just exhibited this avoidance tactic, sit passively and draw attention to the pattern of behaviour they've just exhibited, and then the purpose of the tactic. Then ask for an answer to the question.

Bullies also rely on the denial of others and the fact that when their target reports the abuse they will be disbelieved. Frequently targets are asked why they didn't report the abuse before, and they will usually reply "because I didn't think anyone would believe me." Often they are correct in this belief. Because the bully alternates bullying with charm, depending on his audience, he or she can seem very plausible and is often believed.

Targets of bullying in the workplace often come up against the same attitudes by management when they report a bullying colleague. In a workplace environment, the bully usually recruits one or two colleagues. Sometimes one is a sleeping partner who will back up the bully's denial when called to account.

Serial bullies harbour a **particular hatred** of anyone who can **articulate** their behaviour profile, either verbally or in writing, in a manner which helps other people see through their deception and their mask of deceit. The bully's usual instinctive response is to launch a bitter personal attack on the articulate person's credentials, qualifications, and right to talk about personality disorders, psychopathic personality etc, whilst preserving their own right to talk about anything they choose - while adding nothing useful to the debate.

Bullies hate to see themselves and their behaviour reflected as if they are looking into a mirror.

Meet the bullies

Bullies project their inadequacies, shortcomings, prejudices and behaviours on to other people to avoid facing up to their inadequacy and doing something about it (learning about oneself can be painful), and to distract and divert attention away from themselves and their inadequacies. Projection is achieved through blame, criticism and allegation; once you realise this, understand that every criticism, allegation or claim that the bully makes about his target is actually an admission or revelation about the bully himself.

This knowledge can be used to perceive the bully's own misdemeanours. For instance, when the allegations are of financial or sexual impropriety, it is likely that the bully has committed these acts; when the bully makes an allegation of abuse (such allegations tend to be vague and non-specific), it is likely to be the bully who has committed the abuse. When the bully makes allegations of, say, "cowardice" or "negative attitude" it is the bully who is a coward or has a negative attitude. **In these circumstances, the bully must be made to understand that if damaging and unsubstantiated allegations are made, the bully will also be investigated.**

When the symptoms of psychiatric illness become apparent to others, most bullies will play the *mental health trap*, claiming their target is "mentally ill" or "mentally unstable" or has a "mental health problem". It is more likely that this allegation is a projection of the bully's own mental health problems.

If this trap is being used on you, point out that the bully is projecting his own shortcoming in your defence against disciplinary action or as part of your legal proceedings.

Remember, substantiate all of your claims with exact dates, details of specific incidents, copies of emails, and don't hold back on defending yourself because you feel that you are stooping to the bully's low level of conduct. Your job and reputation could be on the line.

It can be a key identifying feature of a person with a personality disorder or psychopathic personality that, when called to account, he will accuse the person who is unmasking them of being the one with the personality disorder or psychopathic personality from which he (the bully) suffers.

In addition to the advice given above, here are some other tactics you can use to counteract the bullies

Using the exercises for keeping your cool outlined in from page 201 onwards learn to control how much you will allow the bully to damage you personally. With practice, you really can get to the point where you couldn't care less what the prat says or does. Good, that's your **emotional defence** in place.

Keep a note of all his antics. This includes copies of emails sent and received, dates of put-downs, names of witnesses etc. On this point, also keep copies of all thank-you emails and performance reviews. Good, that's a **wealth** of positive and negative **evidence** in place.

You may decide to do nothing; provided you are not being emotionally damaged and remain unscathed; there is nothing wrong with this. Let the bully work towards a premature death from a painful heart attack, while you sail happily through life unperturbed by him.

You may decide to make a formal complaint. If so, use your company's grievance procedure and put your complaint in writing. You may be in a fragile state. Put that to one side while you write your grievance. Make every sentence a statement of fact and substantiate it with an example (it's the *back-it-up-or-shut-up* principle).

Meet the bullies

****

Example

On 22 November 2004 at 2pm, Harold stormed into my office. I was on the phone to a client. He cut off my call and proceeded to shout at me. His exact words were *"Why the hell did you give credit to this loser company? We don't want them as a client, you moron!"*

He threw an unpaid invoice at me and marched out of the room again. I was very shaken and given no opportunity to respond.

Harold is not my direct manager. My direct manager told me he knew nothing about the client in question. It turns out that client was brought in by a different part of the business.

Even if I had brought in the client, I must point out that a) I always follow the written procedures set out by the company and enclose an example that clearly illustrates; and b) the employee handbook sets out clearly the company's communication procedure.

I would have expected Harold to approach my manager if he had a complaint and not to come shouting at me. Harold has refused to deal with me in relation to any work since this incident. I am worried my job is at risk.

I attach copies of emails related to this matter.

****

Note: the single incident in this example doesn't constitute a pattern of bullying in itself. However, the subsequent behaviour – freezing out – combined with the incident does. The experience of this employee, added to the similar treatment meted out by Harold to other employees would make a strong case of bullying for him to answer.

Enlist supporters. You shouldn't feel alone and without support when someone mistreats you at work. You'll probably find the same bully has similarly treated others. Be careful when you confide in a work colleague that you are not feeding information to a friendly viper.

Avoid waiting too long before making your concerns about bullying known.

What are the sources of employment law in Ireland?

In some countries, including some of the new EU member states, employment law is embodied in a single uniform code of rules, often known as a Labour Code. This is not the case in Ireland, where employment law draws from a number of different areas of law that impact the relationship between an employer and employee. Whether you are an employer or employee, if you find yourself in a situation that could end up in a legal dispute, seek expert advice as soon as possible.

There are **four** main sources of employment law in Ireland. These are:

Common law, ie judgement law, developed over many generations of court decisions.

Legislation and statutes passed by the Oireachtas. EU directives are transposed into legislation in each of the EU member states and there will be some variation in detail from state to state. The Organisation of Working Time Act is a good example; in the UK employees can opt out of the Working Time Regulations (although the EU wants this to change).

Terms of a **contract of employment**, including the accompanying documents such as a company's employee handbook, may be relevant in a dispute.

The Constitution of Ireland, which guarantees the fundamental rights of individuals. Any actions carried out by an employer that would have an impact on those rights must be in strict accordance with constitutional and natural justice.

The *three main types of actions* that an employee takes against an employer are:

1. Claim civil damages for personal injuries sustained in the course of employment

This claim would be take in a **civil court**, not an Employment Tribunal. The claim would typically include allegations of one or all of:

Negligence
Breach of contract
Breach of statute

2. Claim for a wrongful or unfair dismissal

A *wrongful dismissal* is the common law remedy in the civil courts for a *breach of the terms of an employment contract*. Like all breaches of contract law, you can bring a claim for wrongful dismissal in the civil courts within 6 years of the breach of contract. The upper limit on the potential award will depend on the loss you suffer and also the court in which you take the case. The District Court can award a maximum of €6,350 and the Circuit Court €38,092.

An *unfair dismissal* is a remedy provided specifically by *legislation* for a *breach of entitlements under that legislation* Claims of unfair dismissal must normally be made to the Employment Appeals Tribunal within 6 months of the alleged dismissal. There have been instances where a claim was allowed within a 12-month period. This doesn't make such an extension automatic. Each case is judged on its merits.

An employee has to choose between either the wrongful or unfair dismissal claim; you cannot take both. Your solicitor will advice whether to proceed by wrongful or unfair dismissal depending on your seniority, professional status, length of service with the employer and the terms and conditions of your contract of employment. Particular attention is likely to be paid to the amount of notice your contract entitles you to on dismissal.

You may have noticed reports in the media of cases where an employee seeks an **injunction in the High Court** to prevent his or her dismissal. The purposes of the injunction would be to put a stay on the alleged breach of the contract of employment and maintain the status quo until a trial is held to hear the dispute. This is an expensive route to take. To obtain the injunction, the employee taking the claim has to compensate for any loss the employer suffers as a result of the injunction if the claim fails. This route is really not a run-of-the-mill step to take in solving wrongful dismissal cases.

What is constructive dismissal?

This may apply where you believe you have no option but to resign because your conditions of work have become intolerable. Your claim would be that the employer caused or failed to prevent these conditions, that the resignation was orchestrated and that you were effectively dismissed. So what should you do?

The burden of proof is on you, the employee, in a constructive dismissal claim.

If possible, don't resign yet. Seek expert legal advice first.

You would need to show that you had invoked the employer's internal grievance procedure **before** you resigned and that this failed to resolve the matter satisfactorily.

Remember, if your employer can claim that he was not made **aware** of the problem, then he can argue he was unable to address it. This does not mean you have no case. Each case differs in circumstances and detail and I can't emphasise too strongly the importance to taking expert advice specific to your circumstances.

However, there may be important reasons why you cannot go on the record with why you can no longer endure this particular workplace. Sometimes, these reasons and the importance of them only become clear during a hearing.

The matter will be judged objectively by someone who was not present; the trail of evidence and presence or lack of **reasonableness** and **fair procedure** on both sides will be very important.

Once you can show that the facts forced you to resign, then the burden of proof shifts back to the employer to show that he acted reasonably. It is very important to take legal advice on this.

Acrimony in the workplace can be extremely stressful and at times, an employee will simply quit and see legal advice later. This is the **worst approach** to take. By all means, if you have already taken this course of action, seek advice anyway. However, if you are in the throes of a tough work situation that you sense may worsen, do talk to an employment law specialist for advice on what to do next.

3.   **Claim to enforce statutory entitlements where the employer is in breach of legal rights or protections.**

Compensation can be awarded for a breach of statutory rights as a wrong in itself. This can be the case even where no dismissal has yet occurred or is not alleged, or indeed where no personal injury has been suffered. An example would be the denial of your statutory holiday entitlement.

These three grounds for claims are **not mutually exclusive** and a case could include more than one of these claims. Beware the dangers of a little knowledge in all cases and do seek specialist advice.

What roles do the Employment Appeals Tribunal, Labour Court, Labour Relations Commission, Rights Commissioners and Equality Tribunal play?

The **Employment Appeals Tribunal** (EAT) is a statutory body established to deal with and adjudicate on employment disputes under the following statutes, as amended where appropriate:

- Redundancy Payments Acts, 1967 to 2001
- Minimum Notice and Terms of Employment Acts, 1973 to 2001
- Unfair Dismissals Acts, 1977 to 2001
- Protection of Employees (Employers' Insolvency) Acts, 1984 to 2001
- Organisation of Working Time Act, 1997
- Payment of Wages Act, 1991
- Terms of Employment (Information) Act, 1994 and 2001
- Maternity Protection Act, 1994
- Adoptive Leave Act, 1995
- Protection of Young Persons (Employment) Act, 1996
- Parental Leave Act, 1998
- Protections for Persons Reporting Child Abuse Act, 1998
- European Communities (Safeguarding of Employees' Rights on Transfer of Undertakings)(Amendment) Regulations, 2000
- European Communities (Protection of Employment) Regulations, 2000
- Carer's Leave Act, 2001

The Tribunal consists of a chairman, 21 vice-chairmen and a panel of 60 members, 30 nominated by the Irish Congress of Trade Unions and 30 by Employers' organisations. A secretariat comprising full-time civil servants seconded from the Department of Enterprise, Trade and Employment, assists the administration of the Tribunal.

The Labour Court provides a free, comprehensive service for the resolution of industrial relations disputes and deals also with matters arising under employment equality, organisation of working time, national minimum wage, part-time work and fixed-term work legislation. Its *recommendations* are not legally binding; its *determinations* <u>are</u> legally binding. Briefly, this is how it works.

The **Labour Court** is not a court of law. It operates as an industrial relations tribunal, hearing both sides in *trade disputes* and then issuing *recommendations* setting out its opinion on the dispute and the terms on which it should be settled. While these recommendations are not binding on the parties concerned, the parties are expected to give serious consideration to the Court's recommendation. Ultimately, however, responsibility for the settlement of a dispute rests with the parties. Normally semi-states companies accept the recommendations of the Labour Court; Aer Lingus broke this trend in the summer of 2004 when it rejected the Labour Court's recommendation in relation to cabin crew's contracts of employment.

For most purposes, the **Labour Court** acts as a court of last resort, ie its services are used when all other avenues have been exhausted. However, it also serves as a court of appeal in relation to decisions by Rights Commissioners, Equality Officers and the Director of Equality Investigations.

When dealing with cases involving breaches of registered employment agreements, the Labour Court makes *legally binding orders*. Also, the Court's **determinations** under the Employment Equality, Pensions and Organisation of Working Time, National

Rights and remedies

Minimum Wage, Industrial Relations (Amendment), Protection of Employees (Part-Time Work) and Protection of Employees (Fixed-Term Work) Acts **are** *legally binding.*

The **Labour Relations Commission's** role is to promote good industrial relations in Ireland. Its main services are:

Conciliation service: a voluntary and free mediation service to help employers and employees resolve disputes. The LRC basically referees the search for a resolution to the dispute between the opposing parties. It does so very effectively too, as over 80% of cases are settled.

Advisory service: works with employers, employees and trade unions in non-dispute situations to develop good industrial relations practices.

Rights Commissioner service: operates as an independent arm of the Labour Relations Commission. Rights Commissioners deal with individual disputes and grievances relating to a wide variety of issues, such as unfair dismissals, working time, maternity and parental leave, part-time work. Rights Commissioner decisions are not binding on the parties.

Where to first?

In relation to employment equality, dismissal and discrimination cases, the Labour Court may fulfil both court of first instance and court of appeal roles. In unfair dismissal cases, where individual workers believe that they have been dismissed, or constructively dismissed, on grounds constituting discrimination or victimisation, they may go directly to the Labour Court to seek redress.

The Court's decision in such cases is called a 'determination' and is legally enforceable. In other cases, involving discrimination or victimisation, but not involving dismissal, the complaint is first of all investigated by an equality officer or the **Equality Tribunal**.

The **Equality Tribunal** is an independent quasi-judicial body established in 1999. Its core function is to investigate, and/or mediate, complaints of unlawful discrimination at work under the Employment Equality Act 1998, and to provide legal enforcement and remedies. Either party to a dispute may appeal against the decision of the Equality Tribunal to the Labour Court, and the Court's determination is legally enforceable.

What is a disciplinary/ dismissal procedure?

Within 28 days of signing your contract of employment you must receive a copy of your employer's dismissal/disciplinary procedure. The provisions of this procedure should be known and understood by all employees and management. The objective of such a procedure is to maintain standards and regulations within the company and to provide a fair process for managing misconduct or alleged breaches of procedure. The steps in the company's disciplinary procedure should be followed by both employers and employees and normally includes:

1. An oral warning
2. A written warning
3. A final written warning
4. Suspension with or without pay
5. Dismissal

What are your rights during a disciplinary procedure?
The following employee rights must be upheld at all times:
- You will have the right to know the case against you prior to a formal disciplinary meeting taking place
- You will have the right to reply
- You will have the right to due consideration
- You will have the right to representation
- You will have the right to appeal

When can you apply for legal protection from dismissal?
- If you work at least 8 hours per week
- If you have more than 1 year's continuous service
- If you aged between 16-66

What are 'unfair grounds' for dismissal?

1. Trade union membership (when it is not infringing on working hours)
2. As a result of taking either maternity, adoptive or parental leave
3. If it is due to sexual harassment that has been left unchecked by your employer
4. If you are taking part or involved in any legal proceedings against your employer
5. Age, race, colour, sexual orientation, family status
6. Membership of the travelling community
7. Religious or political opinions

What are 'fair grounds' for dismissal?

1. An incapability for carrying out the work for which you were employed
2. Incompetence or lack of qualifications to do the work for which you were employed
3. Unacceptable conduct as outlined by your employer
4. Redundancy (where an agreed or fair selection procedure is used)
5. A statutory or legal duty requiring you to cease working or for your employer to dismiss you

How do you bring a claim for unfair dismissal?

You must be able to prove that you were unfairly dismissed and that you have worked more than 8 hours per week for a minimum of 1 year continuously. If you meet these requirements you may bring your claim before a Rights Commissioner or the Employment Appeals Tribunal. Claims for unfair dismissal must be brought within 6 months of the dismissal. There have been cases allowed within 12 months but this does not automatically mean such an extension will be granted in every case.

How can you bring a claim for wrongful dismissal?

Claims for wrongful dismissal are made in the civil courts. They are claims for breach of contract and like all breach of contract cases, claims must be brought within 6 years of the alleged breach.

What if your employer suspends you?

Employers should be cautious about suspending employees and ideally should avoid doing so. The circumstances in which suspension is used are:

1.   Pending an inquiry into something. If there are two opposing parties and both are employees, an employer might suspend both, on full pay of course, while the inquiry is conducted

2.   As a disciplinary sanction.

An employer should never suspend an employee prior to a disciplinary hearing. To do so implies that sentence has been passed before the case has been heard and would raise serious doubt as to whether fair procedure had been followed by the employer.

What is a grievance procedure?

A grievance procedure is a procedure that enables you to raise issues with your employer, where you may be dissatisfied or feel you are being unfairly treated. You should be able to raise issues with a particular individual or individuals whose duty is to hear and investigate the grievance and take action if appropriate. The procedure normally allows for the grievance to be taken to another person or level by way of appeal if the initial response by your employer is not to your satisfaction.

Absenteeism is costing your company a fortune

How can you manage absence effectively? There are no legal requirements, but, if you handle absence problems badly, it is more likely that employees could make successful claims to employment tribunals for unfair dismissal.

You should measure absence to find out:

- How much time is lost
- Where absence occurs most
- How often individual employees are absent

Employ best practice in monitoring absence by:

- Obtaining your employees' consent to keep details of individual records of sickness absence, which are 'sensitive personal data' under the Data Protection Acts.
- Keeping accurate attendance records which show individual instances of absence, together with duration, reason and where in the company the absentee works
- Ensuring that records can be easily analysed by section or department, month or year
- Assuring staff that any sensitive personal data will be kept for only as long as necessary and will only be assessed by named departments or individuals
- Making sure that absence measurement figures show the scale and nature of the problem.

Where there is an absence problem, the main categories of absence involved are:

1. Long-term sickness
2. Short-term certified or uncertified sickness
3. Unauthorised absence and lateness

You can reduce absence levels by paying special attention to:

> Working conditions
> Job design
> Payment systems
> Communications and induction and training
> Welfare
> Employee relations
> Health and safety (including stress)
> Flexible working arrangements
> By making it clear that, while you accept genuine illnesses, phantom 24-hour 'flu' is not acceptable. You don't need to be a monster but, really, it is not fair to allow a few skivers off while the rest of the workforce picks up the slack for them.

Deal with short-term certificated or uncertified sickness by:

1. Interviewing employees on their return to work
2. Making arrangements for medicals where necessary
3. Having a policy on the provision of certificates to cover sick absence, although GPs are not obliged to provide patients with certificates for illnesses of seven days or less
4. Ensuring employees are told if their level of absence is putting their job at risk.

Deal with long-term sickness by:

1. Discussing the problem with the employee concerned
2. Considering alternative work or working arrangements, whether the job can be covered by other employees or temporary replacements and how long the job can be kept open
3. Seeking medical opinions from the employee's GP or a company doctor.

Deal with authorised absence or lateness by:

1. Requiring absent employees to phone in by a given time on each day of absence
2. Ensuring that the supervisor has an informal talk with the employee on the day after absence if no explanation is presented
3. Taking disciplinary action if the unexplained absence continues.

What if you get it wrong?

High levels of unauthorised absence, including lateness and certificated or uncertified sick leave, can:

Cause lost or delayed production
Reduce the range or standard of service
Cause low morale and dissatisfaction
Indicate other, more deep-seated problems.

You want some advice on managing your sales team

Regardless of the size of your sales team, it's important that it is managed properly and given direction so each salesperson can fulfil their potential to develop your business. There you go, that finance thing again!

Begin with the basics and develop a sales strategy that everyone is aware of. This should make clear what your objectives are. For example, is the priority to target new or existing businesses? Which products or services are you most keen to promote?

Your staff should be clear on what their roles are within the sales team. It's usual to allocate responsibility so that one member of staff looks after a particular account, product or territory. Such allocation means that customers can build a relationship with a particular account manager.

Use data such as sales-activity reports to keep track of how well your staff are performing and combine these with reviews where you can discuss results face-to-face with them. This gives you the chance to address any problems or issues with which they're concerned.

Feedback from your sales staff can be very valuable in shaping business direction because of the close contact they have with customers. Of all the staff within your business they are likely to have the best idea of what it is that your customers are demanding.

Measure the performance of your salespeople
You recruit salespeople because you want them to make a difference to your business sales. So how do you measure just how well they're doing?

Managing performance

One method is to analyse a salesperson's conversion rates. This is the number of visits, contacts or phone calls it takes to arrive at one sale to a customer. If, for instance, you calculate that it takes a salesperson 25 approaches per sale you have a good basis on which to gauge his or her progress. Likewise, if you employ several sales staff you can assess which of them is performing most effectively.

If you establish that sales targets are being missed you should investigate the reasons. One possible cause might be a lack of effectiveness on the part of the salesperson. However, it might just as easily be caused by one or more of these factors:

- The territory you've given the person to cover is too wide or too difficult
- There is a fundamental problem with the product or service he is selling
- There is a broader slump right across the market

Whatever proves to be the source of the problem, act quickly to remedy the situation. Where appropriate, let your sales staff know that their salesmanship is not the issue.

From time to time, find out what impressions your salespeople are making. You could try conducting a survey of opinions across the customer base, or on a smaller scale calling individual customers to listen to what they have to say. You might also try accompanying salespeople on their site visits to see for yourself how well they're connecting with customers.

Set activity targets for your salespeople

As well as setting your salespeople targets for the number of sales you want them to make, you should set them activity targets. These are all the individual aspects of their day-to-day duties that your sales team will carry out as part of their jobs and which should lead to sales. The theory is that if enough of these activities are carried out, they will significantly improve the likelihood that sales are made.

Activity targets might be:

- Completed phone calls - ask your sales staff to record the number of calls they make that are completed - in the sense that a conversation has been held with the potential customer

- Face-to-face meetings - get staff to record the number of appointments they make with customers where they attempt a sale

- Leads generated - measure how effective your staff is at extracting new leads and generating potential new custom

- Qualified prospects - ask sales staff to let you have the qualified prospects that they have identified. These are people who have been picked out as needing the products or services you offer and who are able to purchase, but who haven't approached you - or been approached.

You need to set sales targets for your salespeople
You need to set clear targets for your salespeople, linked to commissions and bonuses - this motivates them and provides a clear indication of the kind of performance expected of them.

This process is crucial to the success of your business and needs to be closely tied in with the rest of your business strategy and planning.

Be specific when setting targets for sales staff - break your requirements down into different areas, for example:

Managing performance

New sales: work from the projections in your business plan and sales forecasts - these will take into account changing market and economic conditions.

Renewals: selling isn't only about new business; it's also about retaining your existing customers. A typical renewals rate is in the region of 60 to 70 percent.

Lapsed customers: a good salesperson should be able to recover some of your past customers who have not bought from you for some time.

Look at your business and identify the factors driving its profitability. You should use these to drive your sales targets too. Different businesses may require very different targets. For instance, winning 200 new customers in a year might be a poor performance for a supplier of low-margin consumables, whereas recruiting just two new customers might be a very good performance for developer of top-level luxury homes.

Make sure that the targets you set for your new sales staff are reasonable for the territory they've been allocated. Making things too easy may lead to complacency and lost sales, while making them too difficult can lead to poor morale.

When is it time to hire a salesperson?

There is no defined time at which a business must hire a salesperson. Every business has its own requirements, and can be affected by seasonal patterns, as well as the ups and downs of the economy. However, there are certain triggers you might have noticed in your day-to-day business dealings that could indicate you'd benefit from recruiting a salesperson:

Missed opportunities: you might feel frustrated by missing a number of opportunities that could have been taken advantage of by an astute salesperson with well developed skills in this area.

Lack of resources: running a business or department requires you to give your attention to a huge range of issues. If other tasks become more demanding as your business grows, you may find you no longer have the time to look for new business.

New areas: perhaps you've had an idea about a new market into which your business could move - but lack the specialist knowledge to make it happen.

Increasing sales and market share: it's perhaps the simplest reason for hiring a salesperson, but one of the most sensible. Once you've established there's a need for your product or service you need to maximise your possible revenue. A professional salesperson can help you do this.

Whatever the reason, once you consider hiring a salesperson there's one important question you should ask yourself: would you be able to deal with an increased level of sales? It's an essential factor to consider. There is no point paying someone to bring in new customers if you haven't got the resources to meet the demand.

Why should you use an interim manager?

As organisations have become streamlined, they no longer have available the management resources and expertise to deal with unforeseen or exceptional circumstances. Using interim managers gives organisations the flexibility to handle these situations whilst still retaining their new, leaner structures. Before appointing an interim manager, be clear about the purpose and intended contribution of the interim manager. Advantages of using interim managers rather than other resources include:

- Speed of recruitment gives an organisation the flexibility to respond to market forces and to implement key decisions rapidly (days versus months)
- Prevents other management being diverted
- Gives a breathing space to make a well-considered permanent appointment and reduce the risk of making an expensive hiring mistake
- Interims are usually hands-on managers committed to delivering results, with considerable expertise able to transfer both specialised knowledge and ideas on best practice. They are also able to give coaching in general management skills and are happy to help the development of less experienced managers
- Objectivity and loyalty from having no political baggage or personal agenda for advancement within the client organisation. Many (although not necessarily all) interim managers are not seeking a permanent position, so they do not pose a threat to the promotion prospects of others
- Since interim managers are selected for their interpersonal as well as technical skills, they are generally able to gain the co-operation and respect of colleagues and subordinates

- Interim managers may be very welcome where they are involved in start-up activities or newly merged organisations (but don't expect your interim to work 16 hours a day for a rate that covers half that! Most will work the hours, but you do need to pay them.
- Resourcing is often for a fixed period, at a fixed cost.

How long does a typical assignment last?

Assignments vary in duration from as short as one day to as long as two years, and can be both full- or part-time. A typical assignment might last three to six months.

How to find an interim manager

As interim management becomes more widely recognised, there are many individuals and organisations offering this service. Recruitment can take place through the normal channels such as: advertisement, both in print and online media; specialist recruitment agencies; personal contact and networking.

You can find out more about working as an interim in different countries in my *Go Contracting* series of books – see **www.smartmovesatwork.com**

If you are interested in finding out more about how my own interim management services could work for your organisation, contact me directly at ehouston@smartmovesatwork.com

Why all executive roles aren't created equal

Why do successful executives sometimes fail when promoted to positions that appear to be within their ability? According to a new study by Hay, the problem often lies in subtle but critical differences among senior leadership roles - differences that often call for very disparate skills and behaviours.

They found that rapid growth, the flattening and thinning of management ranks, shifting business strategies, and the growing popularity of more dynamic, matrix-structured organisations have dramatically changed the shape of executive roles. Today's top leadership positions, despite many similarities, vary significantly depending on the shape of the role, its proximity to business results, and the level of operational or strategic focus.

There are three unique role types, each of which, depending on its focus, requires a unique set of competencies. These are:

Operations roles: These are what we typically think of as the more traditional line and general management positions. Operations roles are accountable for business results, often through the direct control of significant people and resources. Successful operations leaders are intensely focused on results. They set challenging goals, establish detailed cost-benefit analyses, and aren't afraid to take calculated risks. They also have a thorough knowledge of their organisation and markets. They know the challenges, threats, and opportunities and are highly flexible in addressing them.

Advisory roles: These roles, often labelled "professionals," provide advice, guidance, and support regarding a specific functional area. Although not directly accountable for results, they're frequently responsible for developing broad functional capability and the interpretation and application of functional policies. Successful leaders in these roles know the entire organisation inside and out. They also have great people skills and are adept at combining those skills with their understanding of the organization to influence others. They tend to be highly conceptual, drawing on knowledge and experience to create new solutions.

Collaborative roles: Rapidly emerging as a mainstay in today's flatter, matrixed organization, such roles lack the direct authority of operational positions. However, they are nonetheless accountable for key business results, which can be extremely challenging for those who have risen through the more traditional executive ranks. They are highly proactive, extremely flexible, tenacious in seeking out information, and tailor their influence and communications based on the people, situation, and culture.

What's the answer?
While most senior executives need a common, core set of competencies (well over 75% of those studied were good at in-depth analysis, applying concepts, and digging for relevant information) additional competencies may be required depending on the scope and shape of the role. The findings raise serious questions about traditional assessment methods, especially those that overemphasise the qualities of the person and pay too little attention to the critical job requirements. The findings also make a strong case for rethinking how organisations select, develop, and promote their leaders. By better understanding the specific leadership role and the competencies required, organisations can effectively reduce their risks and, over time, improve performance.

You are promoted over existing manager

You are considering a job offer for a new position as director of your function, with the current function manager reporting to you. You need some advice on how to handle the inevitable disappointment of the current head of function, and how to handle his team who are very loyal to him

You are about to be the boss, so act like the boss. You need to show leadership. Be clear about what you expect from your team and communicate that. But first, find out what your team expects from you.

Keep in mind that this team has already been working away together, so its members have a great deal of information that will be useful to you.

Meet each team member individually. I recommend that you open each of those discussions by asking the individual to outline about their career to date and their future aspirations. Then stop talking and **LISTEN**.

You'll find out a huge amount this way, including hints of any obstacles that lie in your path. You'll get to know your colleague, be considerably better informed as a result of each discussion and your team member will be delighted to have been listened to.

Is it really inevitable that the current manager will be disappointed? It may seem a certainty, yet there are often other issues that affect how the current incumbent will react.

An important factor is the reason for this new, higher level, appointment. Has there been a performance issue in the team? If so, the current manager may well be relieved that you will be responsible for solving it.

The key here is to approach the situation with an open mind. Meet with the current head and ask his opinion on certain issues and situations. He has the experience of running the team and is likely to have suggestions and thoughts on how it could be improved. Why hasn't he taken some action before now, you wonder? Not everyone has the capacity to implement change. If this team has been plodding happily along for some time, the existing manager may not have felt sufficiently confident or comfortable to make drastic changes. Or he may not be up to delivering that level of leadership.

Discuss openly with him the situation in which you both find yourself, ask how he wants you to play it and what is important to him. He will not want to lose face, though be prepared for the possibility that he may have no issue with your appointment at all!

Equally, he may have other ambitions and this is a good time to find out what those are. Be careful not to be perceived as keen to see him on his way – out of a job! You can also explain how he could be helpful to you in ensuring that the team meet their business objectives.

Congratulate him on the work he has done to date, the results achieved and the loyalty built up in the team. Explain that loyal people will be most influenced by the relationship they see between the two of you; if the relationship is positive, they will be positive. Undergoing this process forms the basis of a contract where you can both get what you want.

It is quite likely that he may be disappointed. Ensure that he has had whatever feedback he needs about the selection process. And then, get on with the job. Getting your promotion was an achievement. Now show that you deserve it.

Moving on, moving up

Let me out of here!

You handle the marketing for a company that sells data and analytical software to the financial services sector. On paper your job looks exciting but in reality it bores you rigid. You would like to move towards journalism but are shocked at the pay levels. You feel completely trapped, what can you do?

First you need to recognise that "problems" are simply stuck patterns of feeling, thinking or behaving. So instead of dwelling on your desire to move, you either need to move, or take some action to alter your current job in a way that makes it more interesting and enjoyable.

Feeling trapped in your job is not an uncommon phenomenon. There are, however, a number of things you can do. The first and most obvious is to ask yourself why you're only thinking of *one* alternative, which you then discount for financial reasons?

Then, ask yourself how you can make your existing job more interesting. Have you discussed this with your boss? Are there any initiatives or projects you can get involved with?

Next, consider whether you really want to write. If so, *start writing*. Journalism is a tough business, but rewarding. Competition for jobs is intense and you need to build up a portfolio of work, even if it is unpaid.

While you're at it, consider whether it is not also other elements of your life that are boring you. Do you have a social life? Enjoy good conversation? Laugh and have fun? Exercise? Have a partner? Have friends? Do you live to work or work to live?

Are you bored or boring?

Getting ahead without a degree

You have been working for ten years, gaining new skills and experience. What is open to someone with experience, rather than a piece of paper?

Of course, there are plenty of examples of people getting to the top without qualifications, but these days, a degree or at least some form of third level qualification is increasingly important, unless you have gained such valuable experience that an employer wants to hire you for that alone.

In the current recruitment market, qualifications are probably even more important. Yes, there is an abundance of job opportunities. But that doesn't mean a lower standard. Many of the companies growing in Ireland now require more brains than brawn and you'll enhance your chances by consolidating some of your skills and experience in a qualification.

The good news is that now all of your courses can link up. The new National Qualifications Framework is a single, nationally and internationally accepted entity, through which all 'learning achievements' may be measured and related to each other in a coherent way. It defines the relationship between all education and training awards.

The framework comprises **ten levels**, with each level based on specified standards of knowledge, skill and competence. These standards define the outcomes to be achieved by learners seeking to gain awards at each level.

The ten levels will accommodate awards gained in schools, the workplace, the community, training centres, colleges and universities, from the most basic to the most advanced levels of learning. Learning achieved through experience in the workplace or other non-formal settings will also be recognised in the awards.

10-LEVEL FRAMEWORK

1 2 3 4 5 6 7 8 9 10

FETAC

SEC

DIT

HETAC

UNIVERSITIES

LEVEL 1 CERTIFICATE
LEVEL 2 CERTIFICATE
LEVEL 3 CERTIFICATE
JUNIOR CERTIFICATE
LEVEL 4 CERTIFICATE
LEAVING CERTIFICATE
LEVEL 5 CERTIFICATE
ADVANCED CERTIFICATE
HIGHER CERTIFICATE
ORDINARY BACHELOR DEGREE
HONOURS BACHELOR DEGREE
HIGHER DIPLOMA
POST-GRADUATE DIPLOMA
MASTERS DEGREE
DOCTORAL DEGREE

How can you change from colleague to boss?

You have recently been promoted to a position where you manage five people who were your colleagues. How do you manage the transition from contemporary to boss?

Your question presumes that a transition is necessary, which may not be the case. However, from your viewpoint, make a list of what you perceive to be your current behaviours with these individuals and this group. In your opinion are you friendly or over-friendly, dominant or dominated? Are you better socially or keeping to business issues?

Then make a list of the behaviours you feel you would need to change to be an excellent manager. What are appropriate behaviours and inappropriate behaviours in your new role? For example, you may decide it would be useful to be more decisive or less accepting of negative comments from team members.

When you look at the two lists, current behaviours and the desired behaviours, you will start to see more clearly the transitions you think you need to make.

Now for the really important part. Ask the individuals you are managing. How can I best help you in your career? What do I need to do to get the best out of you? What should I absolutely not do?

Getting these things clear from the start forms a contract with your team. You look good and they look great. Once you've carried out these two exercises you will be in a much better position to determine what specific transitions, if any, you should make.

Remember, you are the boss now, so act like the boss. Show some leadership by setting a good example.

You've been turned down three times for promotion

You considered yourself the ideal candidate for each position and were pipped at the post every time. You've no idea why. What should you do?

Well, you get marks for tenacity. The fact that you have no clue as to why you didn't succeed is a symptom of a lack of feedback in the organisation.

So first, get feedback that lets you know specifically where you are in the eyes of those making the promotion decisions. "I am committed to a management career here, what would I have to do in order to be promoted next time?" is a good starter question. Listen to the answer and separate issues of *competence* from issues of *behaviour*.

"You don't have experience in xyz systems" is a competence issue so ask yourself, and the organisation, "How do I best develop this competence?" From here you can start to set goals and make development plans.

An answer such as "You would need to be more dynamic," is a behavioural issue. Because we all have an individual understanding of what constitutes "dynamic" behaviour, you need to get specific. Ask "how would you know I was being more dynamic? What would I be doing? What would I be saying that would let you know?"

The answers you get now, such as, "being in earlier in the mornings, producing reports on time", or whatever, are things you can take responsibility for and can set goals and make plans.

At the very least you have set up a dialogue based on constructive two-way feedback, so take the mystery out of your situation and ask.

A final tip – be seen to implement the suggested changes.

179

Shifting from public to private sector

You have decided to move into the private sector after years in the public sector. You believe your skill set will add most value in financial services. You have the skills to make the transition and are not deterred by agencies telling you that you are too old (39) or in the wrong area. You are an engineer, a qualified accountant and hold a PhD. Your studies for the latter two qualifications were paid for by your public sector employer.

Agencies tend to be driven by the strict parameters set by their clients and this does not often allow them to think laterally when addressing recruitment. Also, as the public sector offers greater job security, better pensions and the benefits of benchmarked salaries, some agencies may query why you want to leave. I presume you have used up all of your leave of absence options?

To move things forward, you need to put yourself directly in front of the decision makers so that you have the opportunity to persuade them of your talents. To get to the decision maker you need to build a network. Think of all the people whom you have encountered in your career and social life and who may be able to help now. There is a good chance that you have got a decent network you can tap into. Make them aware of what you want to achieve, seek their advice and find out if they can put you in touch with individuals in your target organisation.

If your contacts cannot help, then write directly to the recruitment director or the Head of the Department of your chosen area, sending your CV with a short covering letter. Follow up that letter with a phone call - this is your opportunity to explain your interest and talents.

You may have to kiss a lot of frogs to find a prince so be prepared for rejection, but also use the opportunity to ascertain if that person knows who else might be able to help you and if they have any suggestions on how you might achieve your goal.

You've made a mistake. Should you admit it?

What's better? Admit to the mistake and get on with fixing it? Blame someone else? Deny all knowledge?

So, you've made a mistake have you? Was it a clanger? Mmm, well that makes you – a HUMAN BEING!

The ability to take responsibility for mistakes and indeed to apologise has nothing to do with your capability; *it's about mentality.*

Real leaders can admit it when they're made a mistake, even though it means putting their reputation (and possibly even their job) on the line.

It sends a message that you are strong, unafraid of risks and don't need to pretend you are perfect. Let that mentality be reflected in how you behave.

Don't be melodramatic in your apology. Something along the lines of "xyz has happened, I apologise for that (or I take responsibility for that) and here is what I am doing to rectify it" in a calm voice will usually do the trick. Only a very mean-spirited person will then focus on the mistake instead of the remedy, but they do exist. Don't let their malevolence trouble you.

You have choices once you've had a failure: disappear from sight, play it safe and basically never be heard of again, or have another go.

I'm in the have-another-go camp. Go on, bounce back.

You want to gain some power at work

What flashes into your mind? The image of some bloodthirsty political animal yelling at subordinates, telling tales about relationships that are not working and basically stopping short of little as they scramble their way to the top?

Well, such people do exist and in some organisations they are the *only* people who survive and thrive. As a result, some managers and workers really dislike power politics.

But you can have power without sacrificing your integrity. Power is a positive thing; it enables you to have the freedom to influence your environment. With power comes responsibility and you do need to be able to handle both.

When you have no power, it is difficult to imagine what being powerful is like. So, people at the lower end of the hierarchy only see the negative aspects; an endless stream of pressures, responsibilities, power struggles, people being paid 'for doing nothing' and ultimately a raw deal for those further down the ladder.

Gaining power is about survival, to be able to be yourself and have some independence in a competitive world. That means being realistic. *Smart Moves* is not about idealising organisations as they should be. It is about surviving and thriving in organisations as they are. Being powerful is no substitute for being good at your job; think of it as an important element of it.

You can gain power from many different sources. Here are some examples:

Position power: use your position and responsibilities to get people to accept your influence and do what you want them to do. When you do have a position of responsibility, then you must be seen to use the authority and power that go with the job. The boss is expected to act like the boss. This generally means taking responsibility for final decisions. Don't forget to consult and inform. "Nobody asked us" is one of the most common gripes in the modern workplace.

Power over human and financial resources: if you control who is hired and fired, what people earn and other budgets, then you will be accurately perceived as a very powerful person in your organisation.

****

A case of how not to do it

The founder and chairman of a multi-million euro indigenous technology company hung on to the power to veto all hires. This meant 'interviewing' every candidate, despite being absent for weeks at a time in a period of rapid growth to raise funds. In some cases, these final interviews were real enough, however at one time, 50 appointments had to be delayed so they could get 1 minute each (time to say hello, give them a quick once-over and to ask them who they knew). The undoubted benefit to each of these 50 individuals of meeting a very charismatic person was wiped out by the wasted time to the business as it was forced to wait for these new hires to start.

****

Power from doing the dirty work

Rationalisation and redundancies are among the toughest decisions a manager has to make; hardly surprising that many try to steer clear of them. However, you will increase other people's perception of your power if you make the tough decisions yourself instead of delegating them. You'll find guidelines for communicating difficult decisions and dealing with the emotional fallout later in this book

Expert power

Your power may derive from having a special skill. Are you expert in IT, finance, a technical field (engineering for instance), marketing? If you possess skills other people do not have, you can use these skills to influence others. This presents a good reason to continually look at how you can add to your skills and knowledge, perhaps by taking additional qualifications.

****

An abuse of ' expert' power

An ambitious administrator, a friendly viper, joins a multi-million euro firm with limited in-house IT expertise, just a quiet young man who is afraid to open his mouth and anyway is somewhat less skilled in IT than he has given the employer to believe.

The MD hasn't a notion of IT and can just about send an email; he freely admits his lack of knowledge in this area.

His secretary has some general IT knowledge, gleaned from watching IT professionals and typing up their work. In her own mind, she is an IT expert. She doesn't bother trying to learn anything from the company's pricey external IT vendors, as she knows more than them already.

She persuades her boss of this simply by announcing it and criticising all of his IT suggestions. The MD likes confident people. And he's had some turnover of admin staff, so he's quite pleased now.

This particular MD has been badly stung in the past and in all areas of his business now insists on contracts that some might consider extreme. For instance, he makes the directors of his main IT supplier sign a contract giving him title to their homes in certain circumstances. Whether this contract would hold up in court must be questionable, since the limited company providing the services is a separate legal person from its directors. But, hey! it keeps the customer happy. They sign.

Moving on, moving up

It's an open secret that this MD has the hots for his new administrator. His business is worth a fortune to the external vendors. Under normal circumstances, they wouldn't hesitate to point out a problem. But the personal situation combined with the contracts-from-hell makes them reluctant. So the external vendors make no comment.

They know she has some highly desirable skills, just not in IT. They are careful to take responsibility only for their contracted work, which she can't harm. Their part of the IT project works fine.

To be fair, she manages a couple of administrative IT tasks just fine.

Friendly Viper takes her responsibilities very seriously and, among other high-handed missives, fires off a *Corporate Paper Clip Directive* to the company's senior management forbidding them to put the branded paper clips to anything other than business use. Each of the recipients of this directive has at least 15 years senior management experience. They say nothing.

The self-proclaimed IT expert takes charge of the company's new website. The old one wasn't too bad actually, and could have been transformed in-house in two days.

The external vendors feel slightly guilty (they admire this MD very much, he's a very high achiever). Still, they say nothing about the public face of his company – its website – which now looks cheap and tacky, is technically broken and full of mistakes, though websites are very, very simple to get right. More tack is added regularly.

Some potential new clients don't bother looking at the site; it's a very good company in many ways and can deliver what they want. Others do look at the site and it deters them from finding out more about the company. The field sales team receives this feedback but says nothing to protect their jobs.

Nobody tells the MD. But nobody helps out the 'I'm-loved-by-all IT expert' either. It's a classic case of a friendly viper getting her comeuppance.

The end result? The website continues to deteriorate to a point where it reflects very little about the reality of the company (it looks like a one-man-bandit slot machine), the silence is maintained, the MD remains unaware of the public hatchet job that has been done on his company's image and has no reason to believe it is anything other than brilliant and the 'IT expert' pushes away for more promotion. She gets it.

Most of the senior management leaves over time.

Of course, this story didn't actually happen in any company that I know of. But it could.

****

Information power

This could mean having the latest information that is useful to colleagues and the organisation. Knowledge is power. If you are in a support (non-revenue earning) role, you could still have a lot of knowledge power. In finance for instance. Use it well and avoid the temptation to behave like a fat dictator.

Power of having vision

The ability to come up with good ideas and to fight for them passionately is a great source of power. However, don't waste your power by fighting for lost causes! Ryanair's Michael O'Leary is a good example of how you can impress people by having a clear vision of the future. He knows what he wants for Ryanair and has worked out how to get there. He lives his vision.

Referent power

This kind of power comes from other people's desire to be like you, with you or to identify with you. They see you as a role model. This kind of power can be very magnetic.

Referred power comes from being associated with someone powerful. For instance, you might be close to the managing director. This gives you referent power, as you will be seen as someone whom it is useful to be associated with. In turn, your subordinates will enjoy some referred power through their relationships with you.

We can all think of people who abuse their referred power. However, you can use referred power in a constructive way. If you are aware of a senior person's support for something you are trying to achieve, make others aware of that support and it will strengthen your case.

Be aware of the downsides to too much referred power. Who wants to be seen as a name-dropping snake? More seriously, if you've hitched your wagon too closely to a rising star who then falls spectacularly, you could lose your gloss too.

Power of persuasion

Good communicators derive power simply from their ability to be articulate, present their ideas clearly and to persuade. Keep this in mind when you are under pressure. If you can keep your cool, you will keep your power. Lose your head and you will not.

You want to build a good network of contacts

Well get out there! Make friends throughout the organisation and not just in your own department. Increasing your knowledge of your organisation's business will help you enhance the way your role or department fits it and will allow you to make contacts across the organisation. Get to know, and make yourself known to, colleagues as soon as possible when you start in a new job. You can do this informally by stopping by their offices or workstations. Not everyone will have time to chat, but generally people will appreciate your efforts. Except the bullies.

Despite an initial good start, you find yourself out of the loop at work
Informal networks change all the time. Once you have gained entry to the network, then you need to stay in it. A key point is not to challenge the values and habits that are sacred to the network.

You want to build a long-term alliance
Stay in touch with people even when you are not looking for a particular favour. While it is acceptable to get in contact when you want something, if it is the only time you bother talk to that person, they will feel used. Get in the habit of building long-term alliances.

You've been called to an impromptu performance review

You were recently summoned by your manager for an impromptu "performance review". She had prepared a performance improvement plan with criticisms of your work, steps to be taken and a month's deadline for improvement, or disciplinary action would begin. You were asked to sign it, and did so, despite rejecting some of the criticism. What are your rights?

There is no legal requirement for you to sign such documents and if you disagree with the accuracy of their contents you should request any amendments that you consider necessary.

The fact that you have already signed unconditionally may be seen as an acceptance of your employer's criticism. As such, if you don't accept the criticisms, you may be wise to invoke your company's grievance procedure and formally register your discontent with having signed the document. Act on this without delay.

At the grievance interview you will be able to discuss your concerns with the employer and may be able to persuade them to amend the document so that it better reflects your performance.

If the employer refuses to amend the document, the grievance documentation will serve as evidence of your complaint at this early stage. If you are later dismissed and bring a claim at an employment tribunal, this record may assist you in stating your case.

In any event, you do have statutory protection from unfair dismissal (provided that you have worked continuously for your employer for at least one year). If your employer were to dismiss you after the one-month deadline, that dismissal would probably be held by the Employment Appeals Tribunal to be unfair, regardless of whether or not you signed the performance improvement plan.

This is because, where an employer considers there are problems with an employee's performance, the employer should follow a **fair procedure** before dismissing an employee.

Generally, that will involve several stages, for example, an oral warning, a written warning, a final warning and then dismissal. The employer must also identify the areas of under-performance, give the employee an opportunity to improve and provide the employee with extra training if necessary.

If you have not been employed continuously by your employer for one year, you have no statutory protection for unfair dismissal and provided that your employer gives you the correct contractual and statutory notice, they may dismiss you, and you will have no legal recourse (except perhaps in a discrimination claim).

It appears that you are at the beginning of this process. Therefore your employer may begin the disciplinary procedure if they consider that you have failed to improve by next month. Unless you have been employed for less than a year, it is unlikely that your employer will dismiss you at that time.

The most likely disciplinary sanction at that stage is a first written warning and, as explained above, your employer should attempt to assist you in developing your ability to reach the required standard. If you do become involved in any disciplinary proceedings you should ensure that prior to a hearing you are fully aware of the allegations against you, and you have had an opportunity to prepare your case in response. You should also ensure that you have the opportunity to be accompanied at the hearing by a representative (either a fellow employee or an appropriately qualified union representative).

Your boss wants to get rid of you

You are having difficulties with your boss. Last month, out of the blue, she accused you of being "lazy and taking pleasure in causing disruption," and said if your attitude didn't improve, she would commence dismissal proceedings. You asked for a meeting with HR and your boss, at which HR said there appeared to be no way forward. You feel you've been wronged and everyone now wants to leave it be.

You have two courses of action. You can stay and try to resolve the situation, or you can leave and get another job.

You may also have a grounds for claiming constructive dismissal, but you should only contemplate this if you have real difficulties finding alternative employment.

In order to try to resolve this situation, you have already involved HR who you feel have been ineffective. I'd say what has happened is that HR have privately taken your silly manager to task for having exposed the company to a constructive dismissal claim!

You are now entitled to invoke your employer's grievance procedure and take the matter to your boss's manager as a formal complaint. Whether this will improve the situation depends on him or her, but it doesn't sound like you have much to lose.

Indeed, I strongly recommend you invoke the disciplinary procedure; it will force the company to address your boss's poor management and will insure you against any similar tricks by her in the future. She is the one who should now be subject to disciplinary proceedings; don't lose any sleep over her discomfort.

On the other hand, it would appear that trust has been broken between you and your boss and sometimes it just isn't possible to rebuild a working relationship once this has happened.

Though it can be done if both parties want the relationship repaired.

If you think the relationship is irretrievably broken, consider moving to a new employer or put pressure on your existing employer to offer you an alternative job in your current company. Or they could move the dodgy manager – they'll have gotten this message loud and clear through the grievance procedure.

A final note on the constructive dismissal issue. It never hurts to take legal advice at this stage (though the going rate for a good employment solicitor is about €300 an hour – expensive, but worth it if you need the help); that way, if the situation worsens at a later stage, you'll know where to go.

Your career has suffered since the boss made a pass at you

Your career has stood still since the Chief Executive made a pass at you at the Christmas Party. On the advice of your line manager, you did not inform HR, since the pass was only verbal. Your subsequent pay review has been very poor and your previously rosy prospects have dried up. You want to leave, but are reluctant to resign without another job. Friends have suggested you now approach HR and tell them what happened in connection with your poor pay review and hope for a voluntary redundancy package.

Let's look at this both from the smart move perspective and the legal perspective.

If you look at this in terms of making the smartest move for *you*, then try to be clear in your own mind about what it is you want. If your wish is to leave the company and get a pay-off, talk to a solicitor before you speak to HR.

Look seriously at the job market. If you find something that fits, you may decide to simply change jobs and leave this unpleasant situation behind you.

If you do find the market really tough, that will shape your conversation with HR or the solicitor.

If you look at this from a **legal** perspective, the first point to consider is what evidence you have linking your unsatisfactory pay review and a reduction in your prospects with the pass made at you by the Chief Executive at the Christmas party. The following factors may be relevant:

1) The extent to which the Chief Executive would have involvement in your individual salary review.

2) Whether your salary increase was significantly less than comparable colleagues.

3) Whether any concerns have been expressed regarding your performance during the course of the year.

If you are able to establish a cause or connection between the incident at the Christmas party and your pay review and subsequent loss of opportunities this would represent a clear case of sexual discrimination.

However, this may prove difficult to substantiate. If you consider that the evidence is there it would be appropriate to raise this issue with HR. You may also wish to consider initiating proceedings under the grievance procedure.

As you describe it, it seems that the incident at the Christmas party was less significant than the subsequent pay review and loss of career opportunities. In any event it would generally carry less weight to raise an issue several months after it had taken place, than if you were to do so immediately. That's not to say you would not include this incident as evidence along with other matters in a complaint.

However, as previously indicated the real issue here is the pay review. This should form the central plank of any grievance.

You hope to obtain a redundancy package. Strictly a redundancy package is only available if your job ceases to exist. Whether it would be at all possible to achieve some form of negotiated settlement is impossible to predict.

You need to consider the extent to which you are prepared to raise the profile on this issue. You could initiate tribunal proceedings if the matter is not resolved internally.

However, you would need to commence such proceedings within six months of the act complained of. In this case it may be possible to argue that the discriminatory act is a continuing one and the time period does not run from the initial salary review.

Your career has suffered since the boss made a pass at you

It may also be possible to argue that any failure to take your grievance seriously or remedy any unfavourable treatment was in itself a discriminatory act.

You need to think carefully before raising the profile of this matter. Whilst an Employment Appeals Tribunal would take your claim seriously there is always the risk that publicity of this nature may have a detrimental impact on obtaining subsequent employment. Take some legal advice.

Eugenie Houston's

Working and Living
in America

www.smartmovesatwork.com

A question of time

Can you break your notice period?

You have been offered a new job but you're on three months' notice. Your new employers are not keen to wait that long. Can you be made to stay the full three months?

Your employer cannot *force* you to work out your notice period. However, if you are contractually bound to give three months notice and you fail to do so, your employer is entitled to sue you for breach of contract.

How your employer reacts will depend on your level of seniority. If you are in a junior to middle level role, your employer is likely to be simply annoyed and may refuse to give you a positive reference. But there are additional options open to the employer.

Your employer can claim damages, for example, for the cost of arranging a replacement to carry out the work you would have done during your notice period (less what it would have paid you), or, if no replacement is available, for the value of work lost by your refusal to work during this period.

Your employer may also bring proceedings against your new employer (or include them as a party to proceedings against you) for inducing you to breach your contract.

In practice it is rare for employers to sue employees because it is not worthwhile financially. However, depending on the circumstances, the new employer may be at risk from legal action.

I advise that, on resigning, you negotiate with your present employer to try and agree a shorter notice period, rather than risk possible legal proceedings.

Finally, quite aside from any legal implications, you may also wish to consider how your intended actions may reflect on your likely loyalty to a new employer.

Do you have to work these long hours?

You have been working more than 60 hours a week for your company. Is your company at fault?

The Organisation of Working Time Act sets out statutory rights for employees in respect of rest, maximum working time and holidays. The maximum average working week is 48 hours. Averaging may be balanced out over a 4, 6 or 12 month period depending on the circumstances. The 48 hour net maximum working week can be averaged according to the following rules:

- For employees generally - 4 months
- For employees where work is subject to seasonality, a foreseeable surge in activity or where employees are directly involved in ensuring continuity of service or production - 6 months
- For employees who enter into a collective agreement with their employers which is approved by the Labour Court - 12 months

Every employee has a general rest entitlement as follows:
- 11 hours daily rest per 24 hour period
- One period of 24 hours rest per week preceded by a daily rest period (11 hours)
- Rest breaks - 15 minutes where up to 4 and a half hours have been worked; 30 minutes where up to 6 hours have been worked which may include the first break

I'd recommend trying to resolve this amicably with your employer, as this legislation is not policed well.

The end of your probation period has passed unnoticed. Good sign or bad?

You joined your employer 8 months ago with a six-month probation period. You have not received a confirmation letter or any employee benefits that one would normally get at this stage in your company. Where do you stand legally in relation to notice period and pay if you were to get fired or leave for another job?

Firstly it would be advisable to look at the term of your contract/offer letter relating to your probationary period to see how it is worded.

Does it state that you were subject to review during and at the end of your probationary period? It is likely to say that your performance should have been reviewed during the six-month period and that during this period either party (ie you and the employer) could terminate the contract on giving the other party a particular period of notice. It is usual to increase this notice period at the end of a probationary period.

In this instance your employer has not confirmed your contract. In the absence of this express confirmation, it is certainly arguable that your employer's inaction implies such confirmation. Accordingly if your offer letter states that you are entitled to a longer notice period after six month's work, this is what you can argue you are due if your employment is terminated.

Once you have one year's service with your employer you have better rights as an employee than you do now. In particular you have the right not to be unfairly dismissed. This means that an employer has to be very careful when terminating the contract of an employee with more than one year's service as the employer could face a claim for unfair dismissal in the Employment Tribunal.

When you say that you are not receiving all the benefits to which you believe you are entitled, I presume you are referring to medical cover and other similar schemes that are open to employees after a certain period of service.

As the situation stands I would approach your employer and ask to discuss the matter. You should say that you understand that your employment has been confirmed in view of the fact that the employer has not said otherwise and that you would like to discuss the benefits due to you. You may find that this is simply an oversight.

If your employer says that your probationary period has been extended then you should argue that you have never been informed of this position and that this is their oversight. Your employer has failed to take the necessary action. It will be very difficult for them to argue otherwise. Though if they try, it would suggest the relationship is on rocky ground.

Finally, if your offer letter/employment contract does not expressly state your notice period, you will be entitled to the statutory minimum notice, which is one week for your length of service.

Good communication, handling stress and keeping your cool

You may be one of those lucky people who breezes through life and work without a care in the world. I'm delighted for you if you are!

However, the reality is that you probably invested in this book because you are not entirely happy at work, due to some fairly benign matter that has niggled under the surface or an extremely serious situation that needs urgent attention, because you are unhappy with the way in which you are treated, or because you feel you simply are not getting results.

Or you may already be slap-bang in the middle of a traumatic workplace crisis. Without exception, every person I speak with who is experiencing this kind of turmoil focuses on the **injustice** of it all. And they have a very valid point. It is *not* fair to be constructively dismissed after ten years with a company (or ever), or to be lied about or bullied or discriminated against.

But I want you to think hard about whether this makes you a victim or a target? Is this something you can survive (ok, maybe with a few emotional scars) or will this destroy your life? The answer is that it can go either way.

To some extent the outcome is determined by the extrinsic measure of 'justice' that you are seen to receive (eg a payoff, good reference, better job).

But long after everyone else has forgotten about your experience and assumes you have gotten over it, the pain of a severe career setback is like any other major emotional trauma and can take a long time to recover from.

Unless, that is, that you accept that you are **not a victim** at all. Yes, you may be the **target** of some appalling behaviour and should and can address this. But don't let it ruin your life.

So what can you do to prevent lasting damage? Well, you'll hear plenty of "you'll get over it", "don't let it bother you", "just forget all about it/ them and move on with your life", "time heals".

All very well-intentioned of course. But leaving a negative experience behind you is not always as easy as that.

What tends to happen in an extremely stressful work situation is that fear freezes you. First, there is the shock that anyone would treat you in this way, given your commitment, dedication, achievements and so on. It can feel as though you are being betrayed by 'family'. You revisit conversations, incidents, searching for something that you have done 'wrong'. You start to blame yourself and search for reasons for the situation.

Without realising it, you could spend hours of your day thinking about the situation and dream about it at night. You can't sleep, gain weight, are constantly worried and prone to panic attacks.

To minimise the damage and scars a workplace crisis can inflict, you need to have concrete strategies for dealing with it.

In the pages that following you'll find strategies for:

1. Determining what percentage of your life you want to devote to worrying about work
2. Dealing panic attacks
3. Beating worry and negativity
4. Helping a colleague or friend in distress, possibly suicidal
5. Thoughts from someone who lost a relative to suicide. This is not a strategy in itself but if you are contemplating self-harm, please read this.

How much of your life do you want to allocate to (worrying about) work?

Remember when you were a kid? Did you ever think about what you wanted to be or do when you grew up? Did you ever put a worry or setback out of your mind because in the future you would be able to do whatever you liked, whenever you liked? You'd have your own money, control over your life and nobody could tell you what to do?

Then one day, many years later, it slowly dawns on you that the future you dreamed of is actually here, you're living it!

All too fast, it's Saturday morning *again*.

That's right. Time is passing. You're getting older. You start to reflect on your life so far. You may be delighted with the way you've lived and where you are now. Or, you may feel that you've missed something.

Do you want to feel that doubt still in 10 years' time?

If not, then it's time to start limiting the amount of time wasted on people and things that mean nothing positive to you. This does not require a lengthy exercise in navel-gazing. Much simpler than that. This book focuses on smart moves at work, it is not about telling you how to live your life.

Here is a simple exercise to determine how much time you spend on work and work-related activities, how much it means to you and how much of the remainder of your life you plan to devote to work.

- What age are you now?

- What age can you expect to reach? Average life expectancy for most of us is 80. What about your relatives? Is there longevity in your family? What age can you therefore reasonably expect to reach?

- Now subtract your current age from the age you could realistically reach

- How many years do you reckon you have left?

- If you're 35 now and hope to reach 80, that leaves you 45 years to go

- Now, work out how much time you spend on different activities

- Rate how important each activity that you have listed is to you

- If you like the mix as it is, then great

- If not, then identify which part you want to change and address it

Let's take the example of Jim. He is 35, his grandparents lived to 85, both his parents are fit and healthy and intent on being around for some time left. They are fitter than he is actually. Jim reckons he has 50 years left. This is a simple exercise, not an actuarial report, so we'll leave aside holidays and other variations. By all means, factor in as many variables as you want to yourself. Based on his current lifestyle, the table opposite shows how Jim is likely to spend the next 50 years.

What, has Jim invented a longer day? 28.5 hours per day?

What is actually happening is that he spends so much time worrying - an exercise that produces only wasted time – that it impinges on his other activities. Since there are only 24 hours in a day, and worrying demands your full attention, this means Jim is spending less productive time on his other activities than he thinks.

Yet, according to this calculation, he is putting a 118% effort into his life.

If you subtracted the 5 hours wasted daily on worrying, Jim's day would only be 19 hours long, 79% of what it could be. You might say that Jim is making over 118% of effort to get just 79% of a result. At rate he is going, he will spend over 20% of the remainder of his life worrying. That's 10 out of the next 50 years. Wasted.

Activity	Time Hours p/day	% of day (24 hours)	Hours spent per year	Importance of this activity
Work	8	33.33%	2920	
Commuting	2	8.2%	730	
Playing with children	1	4.1%	365	
Caring for children	2	8.2%	730	
Cooking	0.5	2.1%	182.5	
Eating	0.5	2.1%	182.5	
Sleeping	7	29.1%	2555	
Exercising	0	0%	0	
Housework	1	4.1%	365	
Worrying	5	20.83%	1,825	
Socialising	0.5	2.1%	182.50	
Chatting	0.5	2.1%	182.50	
Other	0.5	2.1%	182.50	
Total	**28.5**	**118.75%**		

Dealing with panic attacks, feeling overwrought and distraught

Experiencing a panic attack is not the same as having a panic disorder. A panic disorder is a condition in which the panic felt by the individual is so severe that it becomes a phobia and professional treatment is required.

If you are in a highly stressful work situation, you may experience panic attacks, even if you have never experienced anything like this before. This doesn't mean you have a phobia, or that you are ill or crazy. You are experiencing a very high level of stress. Symptoms of a panic attack could include:

- Racing heartbeat
- Difficulty breathing, feeling as though you 'can't get enough air'
- Terror that is almost paralysing
- Dizziness, light-headedness or nausea
- Trembling, sweating, shaking
- Choking, chest pains
- Hot flashes, or sudden chills
- Tingling in fingers or toes ('pins and needles')
- Fear that you're losing control
- A 'fight or flight' response that humans feel when in danger. This could include wanting to flee the scene, to remove yourself from the perceived danger

Good communication, handling stress, keeping your cool

Exercise

Take a very deep breath. This will take a few moments. Repeat several times.

Remind yourself that *you*, not anyone else, are in control of how you will be affected. *You* will decide if, and how much, *you* will allow yourself to be upset.

You may be fearful but you will be able to deal with this panic and whatever is causing it. Repeat:

I am **not afraid** of anyone.
I am **not inferior** to anyone else. In fact, I am good, decent person.
I am **indifferent to** other people's **negative opinions** of me.

Repeat this at least 5 times when you feel panic, until the panic subsides. Keep breathing deeply.

Feeling better? Good. You've just proved to yourself that you are capable of controlling how upset and upset you can become.

Worrying becomes a habit. That's all it is a habit. It wastes your time, achieves nothing positive and makes you feel rotten.

Why not substitute this simple and very effective technique for dispelling panic works for the misery of the worrying habit?

Even if you are not currently experiencing panic, practice this technique anyway, so that you can resort to this new habit when faced with a situation that would previously have provoked panic in you.

Daily exercise for beating worry and negativity

On waking, don't scramble out of bed and sprint straight into the day's hurly-burly.

Wake up. Stretch while you are still in bed. Tell yourself: this is a beautiful day. *Sense* something that proves this, eg see your child, the view out the window (even if it is raining), the colour of the sky, hear the birds in the garden, smell the crisp early morning air.

The source of your anxiety may still be prevalent but before you have even risen for the day, your first thoughts have been of the elements of your life that are rewarding. Will this help you with the challenges of the day ahead? Yes, it should. **You are already ahead in the positive thinking stakes and you haven't even gotten out of bed yet.**

So, you know from the previous exercise how to remind yourself that you are unafraid and a good and decent person. Next, identify some people who are in a worse position than you, and some who light up your life.

Do you remember as a child being cited an example of some other child somewhere who was worse off than you, with no toys, or starving? Emotive examples, and important, but remote and detached too.

I don't minimise the work-related stress you are experiencing in any way. The purpose of this is to help you deal with your stress. I want you to visualise an *actual example* of someone whose situation is definitely worse than yours. Is it:

- A parent who has lost a child?
- A child who has lost a parent?
- A child who is terminally ill?

- A two-year old girl in India who spends 12 hours at day gathering stones above a mine? (I saw this recently in a documentary; this little face will remain on my list forever).
- Some poor hostage, chained, caged and terrified, pleading for his or her life?
- A little homeless child with expressionless eyes, clinging to its mother in the street while the crowds hurry past to complete last minute Christmas shopping?
- Someone you know you has suffered a injury that will affect the rest of his or her life?
- An elderly stroke victim unable to communicate?
- A child being physically assaulted in a public place while nobody helps for fear of 'getting involved'?
- (Add your own examples – you don't need a very long list, just one or two that will mean something to you when you need to conjure up the image)

None of the people in this list have any control over whatever events resulted in their situation. They simply could not have prevented it.

Some of them (the children especially) are dependent on someone else to care for them and to improve their lives. Whatever it is that could make his or her situation better, if it exists at all, is within someone else's control.

Your situation is different. Your crisis is work-related. You may not immediately be able to deflect the behaviour directed at you, but you have **TOTAL control** over how it hurts you.

Next, think of the wonderful people in your life. Your list could include:

- Your own child, whose face lights up when you arrive home

- Your spouse/ partner
- Your parents
- Your siblings
- Close friends

Now add the other positives in your life. Are you?

- Fit and able to enjoy exercise (those who have lost the use of their limbs call the rest of us 'TABs' – temporarily able-bodied). Makes you appreciate being able to move, doesn't it?
- Funny
- A good parent
- A good child
- A good friend
- A good cook
- A hard worker
- A good thinker
- Generous with your time
- Creative
- Loyal
- Honest
- Attractive, sexy, a fine thing!

Next, list your achievements.

1.
2.
3.
4.
5.

Now repeat all of these steps in succession:

1. Stop crying if you are in a panic, or feeling miserable. Don't wind down into sobs, just make yourself turn off the crying for now

2. If you are doing this first thing in the morning, stretch

3. Take deep breaths

4. Sense something you enjoy (even if the stimulus for the sensation is not present, visualise yourself sensing that sight, sound, taste, smell, touch)

Tell yourself:

5. I am not afraid of anyone
   I am not inferior to anyone else
   I am indifferent to other people's negative opinions of me

6. This person is worse off then me (visualise one person)

7. I have great people in my life (visualise one or more)

8. I have wonderful talents (visualise yourself in that situation, eg with your child, parent, partner, friend, cooking a delicious meal for family friends, running in the open air, tending your gloriously-scented garden, see yourself simply looking very happy)

9. I have achieved (visualise yourself in the situation)

Did that make you feel good? Do it again if you want. Repeat this to yourself as often as you like, whenever you like, wherever you like. It literally takes a few seconds. As well as first thing in the morning, what about repeating the exercise last thing at night? If you are prone to worry, you may find it helpful to repeat it several times at day.

Every time you feel worry or negativity taking hold, push it out and practice this exercise instead.

Worrying is a waste of time.

Someone you know is suicidal

Research indicates that suicides occur at the peak of a depressive episode. Education, recognition and treatment are the keys to suicide prevention.

Know the warning signs of suicide
Talking about suicide
Statements about hopelessness, helplessness, or worthlessness
Preoccupation with death
Suddenly happier, calmer
Loss of interest in things one cares about
Visiting or calling people one cares about
Making arrangements; setting one's affairs in order
Giving things away

A suicidal person urgently needs to seek professional help

Know what to do
Stigma associated with depressive illnesses can prevent people from getting help. Your willingness to talk about depression and suicide with a friend, family member, or co-worker can be the first step in getting help and preventing suicide.

If you see the warning signs of suicide begin a dialogue by asking questions. Suicidal thoughts are common with depressive illnesses and your willingness to talk about it in a ***non-judgmental*** way can be the push a person needs to get help.

<u>Do not</u> try to analyse, under any circumstances, the cause of the person's depression.

If you are not trained or experienced in helping people who are feeling suicidal, you may appear judgemental. It is not up to you to judge. To appear to do so could push the person to the peak of their depression, where they may harm themselves.

Questions to ask:

"Do you ever feel so bad that you think of suicide?"
"Do you have a plan?"
"Do you know when you would do it (today, next week)?"
"Do you have access to what you would use?"

Asking these questions will allow you to determine if your friend is in immediate danger, and get help if needed. A suicidal person should see a doctor, psychiatrist or professional psychologist immediately. Always take seriously thoughts of or plans for suicide.

Never keep a plan for suicide a secret. Don't worry about endangering a friendship if you truly feel a life is in danger. It's better to regret something you did, than something you didn't do, to help a friend.

Don't try to minimize problems or shame a person into changing his mind. Your opinion of a person's situation is irrelevant. Trying to convince a person it's not that bad, or that he has everything to live for will only increase his feelings of guilt and hopelessness. Reassure him help is available, that depression is treatable, and that suicidal feelings are temporary.

If you feel the person isn't in immediate danger, acknowledge the pain as legitimate and offer to work together to get help. Make sure you follow through. You must be tenacious in your follow-up.

Help find a doctor or a mental health professional. Set up the first call. Be aware that many professional counsellors will want the person to ask for the help themselves. So give the person the phone and the number and, if he wants, privacy to make the call. (You can wait close by).

Go along to the first appointment. You're not going into the appointment. You're keeping the person company on the journey and will be available when they emerge. Don't feel compelled to chatter away on the journey. If your companion wants to talk, then fine. If not, then simply being present will give some reassurance.

Keep in mind that a person who is feeling suicidal is at the peak of a serious depression. They feel as though they are in a deep, black, hopeless hole from which there is no relief except death. You already know the perils of appearing judgemental. By just being present and behaving in a 'normal' way, you may distract the person temporarily from their despair until you reach professional help.

If you're in a position to help, don't assume that your persistence is unwanted or intrusive. Risking your feelings to help save a life is a risk worth taking.

If you are in Dublin, you will find counsellors at the Clanwilliam Institute (www.clanwilliam.ie). If you can't find a similar group near you, contact them anyway and they'll more than likely be able to give you some names.

Smart Moves at Work

Are you thinking of suicide?

This next note is note from me. Someone who lost a much-loved nephew to suicide wrote it.

If you're thinking of suicide you need to know that if you go through with it, your death is not your own, it's not your family's – it 'belongs' to the State.

Whoever finds you has to deal with a terrible scenario. It could be some passer-by on their way to work. They have to deal with the shock, they have to contact the Gardai, deal with the ambulance services, perhaps the fire brigade.

Someone has to answer that knock on the door and go with the Gardai to the hospital morgue to identify you. They have to say…"yes, this is…" They have to break the news to your family. How hard do you think this is?

If you've left a note, your family won't get to keep it. It's evidence; the State keeps it. At best, your family will be allowed to read it and, sometime after the inquest, they'll get a photocopy of your note, not the original.

Is that what you want? To have your last thoughts and wishes left as a photocopy whilst the original is kept in a file in the State Archives?

There will be a post mortem. The hospital staff will do their very best to handle things sensitively and they will. But the results of the post mortem won't be known for months, until the inquest. So in the meantime, your family is wondering why, why, why. Wondering.

Forget the funeral for a moment, we all know how they go because so many of us have to attend them. Keep to the practicalities. Someone has to advise your friends, work colleagues and acquaintances. Ireland being Ireland, it's like a bush fire, word spreads so quickly.

But there are always those people who don't know, and everyday things like post, bills etc that have to be dealt with. Someone has to do it, whether they want to or not.

Then there's the inquest. Eventually. Think about it. What it will be like for your family to get notification. Attend at 2.00pm at such-and-such date at such-and-such court.

And they do. Your family members walk into a courtroom and find 6 other families there. So your death isn't exclusive, it's one of 7 to be dealt with on that day by the Coroner.

So they sit there, listening to the details of 6 other suicides. Waiting until yours is called. And as the coroner gives a verdict and extends sympathy to each family, they get up and walk out.

Until eventually it's your family that's left. Waiting to hear what they already know, but hoping that some extra piece of evidence will throw a light on why you did it.

But you know what? It probably won't. They won't really know much more than when they went in.

It's just that it's now official.

You're dead.

Communicating bad news

In planning for an announcement of bad news or major change, it is wise to anticipate how the employee(s) might react. Losing your job is a shocking and stressful event involving significant loss. People react to such setbacks differently, depending on their personality and other factors. The importance of 'other factors' should not be underestimated.

Predicting how a person will respond is not easy. Although you may have observed that person's reaction to some similar high-stress loss situation, it would be wrong to assume that the person will respond in the same way to this news.

Being aware of the kinds of reactions experienced by other people will help you prepare for what to expect. Following are descriptions of five of the different ways in which how individuals may react and how you should respond.

The reactions described are:

- Where the employee has anticipated the bad news

- Where the employee reacts in an argumentative manner

- Where the employee reacts by wanting to 'escape' the scene immediately

- Where the employee has not anticipated the news at all and, while he may give the impression of having everything under control, is stunned and disbelieving

- Where the employee reacts violently to the bad news

Anticipatory reaction

You have just communicated news of redundancies to an employee who has anticipated the termination announcement and is concentrating on the details of the severance package.

Clearly, the loss of a job is a major trauma. The most common reaction is a combination of defensiveness, anger and other characteristics associated with a normal grieving process, together with an understandable concern for pragmatic issues.

This person:
- Will not be very intense or emotional at this time
- Will concentrate on the details of the severance package and any outplacement services. References are always a concern
- May blame management and the company for the downsizing/ job loss
- Has probably anticipated that the termination was looming and inevitable
- May have hoped to delay the announcement by being absent, in the belief that by missing announcement, they could avoid being officially informed.

DO	**DON'T**
Listen	Make promises
Wait for the employee's response	Get defensive
Repeat the message if necessary	Justify or argue
Keep to the outline of your prepared	Threaten
communication and its details	Discuss other employment
	Sympathise, "I know how you feel"

Good communication strategies

Argumentative reaction

You have told an employee he is losing their job and he reacts by arguing

This person:
- Will argue about every aspect.
- May make threats to get back at the company.
- May talk about consulting a lawyer.
- May threaten to go to the media

DO

Listen

Be patient

Allow open-ended questions

Allow individual to vent feelings

Stay calm and professional

Keep to the outline of your planned communication

Acknowledge the employee's right to pursue legal recourse. This is an example of where advice varies from country to country. In Ireland, fair procedure is of paramount importance. If you are following fair procedure and keeping within the law, then you should have no reason to fear legal action.

DON'T

Point with your finger

React emotionally

Personalise

Use platitudes such as "I know how you feel".

Get defensive

Make promises

Escapist reaction

You have just concluded a communication outlining specific redundancies. One employee announces he wants to leave the building immediately

As a manager, you must try to initiate a dialogue on exactly why he is being let go. Every effort should be made to continue the discussion and help this employee vent his feelings. If this is not done, the individual with escapist reactions is most likely to vent his hurt to others – colleagues, family, other people in the industry, perhaps even the media.

This person:
- Will not vent their feelings at that time
- Will try to leave after your discussion has started
- Will not know what to do next
- Will not understand the terms of the redundancy and employee support package (as they have been focussed on leaving from the moment you mentioned redundancy)
- Will want to talk about their feeling in public

DO
Keep the conversation going
Communicate the details of the redundancy/ support package
Ask open-ended questions
Probe to make sure the employee understands that he will be losing his job and that the department will be closing down
Extract some sort of reaction or feelings, positive or negative
Encourage the employee to review the package on offer
Continue the discussion until you feel very comfortable that the person has a good understanding of the whole announcement, especially their termination package

DON'T

Take for granted that this person is okay

Send this person off while he is still exhibiting 'escapist' characteristics

Stunned and disbelieving reaction

An employee offers no resistance to the news that his employment is terminated

The news he is being let go leaves this person stunned. His ego and self-esteem are so damaged that he appears to have everything under control. If you are a manager handling this termination, you may be deceived into thinking that it has gone quite well. There is a tendency and a desire on the part of the management to believe this person is okay.

Individuals who react in this way are often the ones who to the most damage to the organisation and/ or themselves. They do not vent their feelings and tell themselves everything is fine for as long as they can. Eventually, reality prevails. Their reactions could come two weeks or a month later. Suddenly, something explodes inside them and they become extremely upset and distraught.

The point is that the individual is reacting abnormally well to bad news. It is normal to hurt in constructive ways rather than keep feelings bottled up and pretend nothing is wrong.

This person

- Will offer no resistance
- Will answer your questions 'yes' or 'no'
- Did not anticipate the announcement at all
- Will be subdued, passive, disoriented
- Will not vent any emotion towards you

- Will react by not reacting at all
- Will have had his ego damaged
- Will *imply* that he has anticipated the announcement for some time and is unmoved by the news
- Will appear to have everything under control.

DO

Try to get some sort of reaction and listen to it

Repeat the main messages

Probe to make sure the employee understands that he will be losing his job

Encourage the employee to review the supporting communication and bring questions to your attention

Follow up at a later date to ensure the employee understands and accepts the situation and knows what options are open to him

DON'T

Take for granted the person is okay

Send the person off in a state of disbelief

Violent reaction

An employee reacts violently to news that he is losing his job

It is fairly rare that someone's argumentative response is so intense that it becomes violent. But it does happen. This response may include screaming, shouting obscenities, threatening physical harm to himself, the company or the person who is firing them.

As a manager, your objective in this situation is to allow the person to vent his feelings. Instead of arguing or defending the a company, you should ask questions. What makes him feel he is being mistreated?

Generally, the person will calm down in the process of talking about the situation.

After a couple of days, having had time to think about the situation, he realises it is not to his advantage to do something that will make him unemployable or cause legal problems. He may begin to channel his anger into productive energy.

If you are confronted with a violent reaction, act with caution, both during and following the communication of bad news. If the employee becomes violent, take immediate action to defuse the situation, calling for assistance if necessary. This is an example of why it is always good practice to have two people present on either side.

Key points to remember. This person:

- Will be intense.
- Will scream and shout obscenities.
- Will threaten physical harm to himself, the company or even you.

DO

Isolate the employee away from the group
Stay calm, maintain professionalism
Attempt to take the heat out of the situation
Listen
Ask open-ended questions.
Allow employee to vent feelings.
Keep to the outline of planned communication.
Seek help if needed.

DON'T

Point with your finger
React emotionally
Personalise
Patronise – "I know how you feel"
Get defensive or debate
Make promises
Get argumentative

You want to learn how to manage your anger

You don't get angry all that often. But you always feel bad afterwards when you do. Realistically, you can't get rid of or always avoid the things or the people that enrage you, nor can you change them, but you'd like to learn to control your reactions.

The first thing to acknowledge is that just because you've reacted in a way you later regret on a previous occasion does not mean that you have some sort of serious anger-illnesses. Nor does it mean that you would automatically reaction in the same way in similar circumstances in the future.

All sorts of factors can trigger anger; you may for instance have noticed that Ireland's tragic congestion epidemic has made you a little less tolerant than before.

We all know what anger is, and we've all felt it, whether as a fleeting annoyance, mild irritation or as intense fury and rage.

Anger is a completely normal, usually healthy, human emotion. But when it gets out of control and turns destructive, it can lead to problems - problems at work, in your personal relationships, and in the overall quality of your life. And it can make you feel as though you're at the mercy of an unpredictable and powerful emotion.

Like other emotions, it is accompanied by physiological and biological changes; when you get angry, your heart rate and blood pressure go up, as do the levels of your energy hormones.

Anger can be caused by both external and internal events. You could be angry with a specific person, such as a colleague, or event, such as yet more traffic congestion, or your anger could be caused by worrying or brooding about your personal problems.

227

Memories of traumatic or enraging events can also trigger angry feelings.

On the instinctive, natural way to express anger is to respond aggressively. Anger is a natural, adaptive response to threats; it inspires powerful, often aggressive, feelings and behaviours, which allow us to fight and to defend ourselves when we are attacked. A certain amount of anger, therefore, is necessary for our survival.

On the other hand, we can't physically lash out at every person or object that irritates or annoys us; laws, social norms, and common sense place limits on how far our anger can take us.

People use a variety of both conscious and unconscious processes to deal with their angry feelings. The three main approaches are expressing, suppressing, and calming.

Expressing your angry feelings in an assertive - not aggressive - manner is the healthiest way to express anger. To do this, you have to learn how to make clear what your needs are, and how to get them met, without hurting others. Being assertive doesn't mean being pushy or demanding; it means being respectful of yourself and others.

Anger can be **suppressed**, and then converted or redirected. This happens when you hold in your anger, stop thinking about it, and focus on something positive. The aim is to inhibit or suppress your anger and convert it into more constructive behaviour. The danger in this type of response is that if it isn't allowed outward expression, your anger can turn inward - on yourself. Anger turned inward may cause hypertension, high blood pressure, or depression.

Unexpressed anger can create other problems. It can lead to extreme expressions of anger, such as getting back at people indirectly, without telling them why, rather than confronting them face-to-face, or a personality that seems perpetually cynical and hostile. People who are constantly putting others down, criticising everything, and making cynical comments haven't learned how to

228

express their anger constructively. Not surprisingly, they aren't likely to have many successful relationships. When you read about bully types as described in *Smart Moves at Work*, you'll recognise that some bullies are consumed with anger.

Finally, you can **calm down** inside. This means not just controlling your outward behaviour, but also controlling your internal responses, taking steps to lower your heart rate, calm yourself down, and let the feelings subside.

Some people really are more hot-headed than others; they get angry more easily and more intensely than the average person does. There are also those who don't show their anger in loud spectacular ways but are chronically irritable and grumpy.

Easily angered people don't always shout and throw things; sometimes they withdraw socially, sulk, or get physically ill.

Is it good to lose your cool?

Psychologists now say that this is a dangerous myth. Some people use the theory that it is good to 'lose the head' as a license to hurt others. Exploding with anger can actually escalate anger and aggression and does nothing to help you (or the person you're angry with) to resolve the situation.

It's best to find out what it is that triggers your anger, and then to develop strategies to keep those triggers from tipping you over the edge.

Strategies To Keep Anger At Bay

Relaxation

Simple relaxation tools, such as deep breathing and relaxing imagery, can help calm down angry feelings. There are books and courses that can teach you relaxation techniques, and once you learn the techniques, you can call upon them in any situation. If you are involved in a relationship where both partners are hot-tempered, it might be a good idea for both of you to learn these techniques. A good exercise programme, including some yoga, would be a start.

Changing the way you think

Angry people tend to speak in highly colourful terms that reflect their inner thoughts. When you're angry, your thinking can get very exaggerated and overly dramatic. Try replacing these thoughts with more rational ones. For instance, instead of telling yourself, "oh, it's awful, it's terrible, everything's ruined," tell yourself, "it's frustrating, and it's understandable that I'm upset about it, but it's not the end of the world and getting angry is not going to fix it anyhow."

Be careful of words like "never" or "always" when talking about yourself or someone else. Statements such as "this ******* machine never works," or "you're always 1-minute late" only serve to make you feel that your anger is justified and that there's no way to solve the problem. They also alienate and humiliate people who might otherwise be willing to work with you on a solution.

Remind yourself that getting angry is not going to fix anything, that it won't make you feel better (and may actually make you feel worse).

Logic defeats anger, because anger, even when it's justified, can quickly become irrational. So use cold hard logic on yourself. Remind yourself that the world is "not out to get you",

you're just experiencing some of the rough spots of daily life.

Do this each time you feel anger getting the best of you, and it'll help you get a more balanced perspective.

Angry people tend to demand things: fairness, appreciation, agreement, willingness to do things their way.

Everyone wants these things, and we are all hurt and disappointed when we don't get them, but angry people demand them, and when their demands aren't met, their disappointment becomes anger.

If you are prone to anger, try to become aware of your demanding nature and translate your expectations into desires. In other words, saying, "I would like" something is healthier than saying, "I demand" or "I must have" something. When you're unable to get what you want, you will experience the normal reactions - frustration, disappointment, hurt - but not anger.

Some angry people use this anger as a way to avoid feeling hurt, but that doesn't mean the hurt goes away.

Problem Solving

Sometimes, our anger and frustration are caused by very real and inescapable problems in our lives. Not all anger is misplaced, and often it's a healthy, natural response to these difficulties. There is also a cultural belief that every problem has a solution, and it adds to our frustration to find out that this isn't always the case. The best attitude to bring to such a situation is not to focus on finding the solution, but rather on how you handle and face the problem.

Make a plan, and check your progress along the way. Resolve to give it your best, but also not to punish yourself if an answer doesn't come right away. If you can approach it with your best intentions and efforts and make a serious attempt to face it head-on, you will be less likely to lose patience and fall into all-or-nothing thinking, even if the problem does not get solved right away.

Better Communication

Angry people tend to jump to – and act on - conclusions, and some of those conclusions can be very inaccurate. The first thing to do if you're in a heated discussion is to slow down and think through your responses. Don't say the first thing that comes into your head, but slow down and think carefully about what you want to say. At the same time, listen carefully to what the other person is saying and take your time before answering.

Listen, too, to what is underlying the anger. For instance, you like a certain amount of freedom and personal space, and your employer wants to know what you're doing at all times. If he or she starts complaining about your activities, don't retaliate by painting him as a tyrant.

It's natural to get defensive when you're criticised, but don't fight back. Instead, listen to what's underlying the words. It may take a lot of patient questioning on your part, and it may require some breathing space, but don't let your anger - or a colleague's - let a discussion spin out of control. Keeping your cool can keep the situation from becoming a disastrous one.

Using Humour

Humour can help defuse rage in a number of ways. For one thing, it can help you get a more balanced perspective. When you get angry and call someone a name or refer to them in some imaginative phrase, stop and picture what that word would literally look like. If you're at work and you think of a colleague as a creep, picture a creepy-looking but harmless spider sitting at your colleague's desk, talking on the phone, going to meetings. Do this whenever a name comes into your head about another person. If you can, draw a picture of what the actual thing might look like. This will take a lot of the edge off your fury; humour can always be relied on to help diffuse a tense situation.

You want to learn how to manage your anger

Changing Your Environment

Sometimes it is your immediate surroundings that give you cause for irritation and fury. Problems and responsibilities can weigh on you and make you feel angry at the "trap" you seem to have fallen into and at all of the people and things that form that trap.

Give yourself a break. Make sure you have some "personal time" scheduled for times of the day that you know are particularly stressful.

Other strategies for managing anger

Timing: If you and your manager tend to fight when you discuss things late in the day - perhaps you're tired, or distracted, or maybe it's just habit - try changing the times when you talk about important matters so these talks don't turn into arguments.

Avoidance: If your teenager's pigsty room makes you furious every time you walk by it, shut the door. Don't make yourself look at what infuriates you. Don't say, "well, my child should clean up the room so I won't have to be angry!" That's not the point. The point is to keep yourself calm.

Finding alternatives: If your daily commute through traffic leaves you in a state of rage and frustration, try to find a less congested route or negotiate a different start time with your employer.

Remember, you can't eliminate anger - and it wouldn't be a good idea if you could. In spite of all your efforts, things will happen that will cause you anger. And sometimes it will be justifiable anger. As well as many happy days, life will present frustration, pain, loss, and the unpredictable actions of others.

You can't change that, but you can change the way you let such events affect you. Controlling your angry responses can keep them from making you even more unhappy in the long run.

Is the ability to apologise a sign of weakness or strength of character?

An apology can defuse emotions effectively, even when you don't admit an intention to cause any harm, or accept personal responsibility for the action.

Making an apology may turn out to be one of the least costly and most rewarding investments you can make.

It can happen that some recipients of an apology haven't got the manners to receive it graciously. This shouldn't deter you.

Is it possible to repair damaged relationships in the workplace?

You have had a blazing row with someone whose good opinion you value. You each said things you later regretted. The business relationship ended as a result. Both you and the other person respect each other's abilities and achievements and want to be able discuss working together again. You each have indicated some willingness to do so. You're both embarrassed at having lost your cool. Who should make the next move?

I don't believe in taking a fatalistic attitude to restoring damaged relationships at work or in business. It's usually only too late if the other person is dead.

Yes, it would have been preferable if the damage had not happened in the first place. But sometimes rows and misunderstandings happen and people make mistakes.

If you respect each other and each of you has enough backbone to get over what will be just a few uncomfortable moments in your next conversation, then there is no reason why you can't pick up the relationship and take it forward. Yes, it's true it will not be exactly the same as before, but it could be better.

The funny things about rows like this is that both people involved often have a lot in common and are quite alike. That's partly what holds you back from making the next move to resolve the situation. You know the mortification the other person is feeling or has felt, because you have felt it yourself.

Either party can make the next move. If you happen to be the party with the ultimate power to get the business relationship back on track (ie if you are the one who will be paying the money for any services), then the ball is probably slightly more in your court.

If you feel your former associate can handle it (most people can), use humour. Contact the other person by phone and say something like "I've calmed down now, have you? In this case, I am still interested in discussing our mutual business if you are".

If you have received any indication that the other person's still keen, that should work.

Otherwise, drop them a note along the lines of "I hope business has been good for you since we were last in contact. You've indicated that you would be open to future discussions. I now have a project that may be of interest to you. Please contact me if you would like to learn more about this."

Finally, an apology can be a very powerful statement. Not everyone is comfortable with uttering those little words "I apologise for that" (and swiftly moving on to the next topic). If you can't verbalise your regret, use your actions can convey it for you.

Go on, give it another go!

You want to resolve conflict constructively

Conflict is a natural part of life brought on by our different beliefs, experiences, and values. If not managed carefully, however, conflict can harm relationships. Here are seven steps adults can use to resolve conflict.

Treat the other person with respect
Although respecting the other person during a conflict is challenging, try. Words of disrespect block communication and may create wounds that may never heal. Use your willpower to treat the other person as a person of worth and as an equal.

Confront the problem
Find a time and place to discuss the conflict with the other person. Choose neutral territory and a time when you aren't arguing or angry.

Define the conflict
Describe the conflict in clear, concrete terms. Be specific when answering the 'who, what, when, where, and why' questions.
Describe behaviours, feelings, consequences, and desired changes. Be specific and start sentences with "I," not "you."
Focus on behaviours or problems, not people.
Define the conflict as a problem for both of you to solve together, not a battle to be won.

Communicate understanding
Listen to really understand the other person's feelings
Seek first to understand, then to be understood
Step back and try to imagine how the other person sees things
Explain how you see the problem after you have talked about it
Discuss any changes you have made in the way you see things or how you feel

Explore alternative solutions
Take turns offering alternative solutions. List them all
Be non-judgmental of each other's ideas
Examine consequences of each solution
Think and talk positively

Agree on the most workable solution
Agree to a solution you both understand and can live with
Work to find a "win-win" solution
Be committed to resolving the conflict

Evaluate after time
Work out a way to check on how well the solution is working
Adjust the resolution when necessary

Managing bereavement on loss of a job

For most of us the prospect of losing a loved one is dreadful. If it happens to you, it can feel like the end of the world. Actually, make that 'when', not 'if', as death is one of life's few certainties.

Yet, nobody can ever be fully prepared for the impact of bereavement. Perhaps that is because we don't talk about death? You can help yourself by understanding a bit more about some of the issues and emotions you are likely to encounter.

We do talk more freely these days about the potential loss of a job, due to redundancy or some other reason.

The loss of a job can come as a short, sharp blow, even when there have been warning signs. You form strong bonds in the workplace and feel as though you've lost part of your family when that relationship is severed. It can feel like a personal loss.

When you experience a workplace 'trauma', whether the loss of a job, a rigged performance complaint (or a justified one), dealing with bullying or any situation in which you feel you've been unfairly treated, it is quite normal then to go through a sort of bereavement process.

The following are all common emotional responses to bereavement. They may come after each other, seem completely random or be repeated during the mourning period.

Shock and numbness

Most people who are bereaved report a phase straight after hearing the news in which they feel they are cut off from others. They feel numb and unable fully to take in what has happened. Some people carry on with daily tasks, almost as if nothing has happened. Others sit for hours, feeling as if they cannot move.

Anger and tension

Many people experience feelings of anger after a bereavement. Sometimes in the case of a death this anger comes out as directed

239

at a doctor or nurse who cared for a loved one or at a member of the family. Or even at the dead person for leaving you alone.

In the case of a job loss, the anger may be directed at your manager, your colleagues who survive, the company or at yourself, perhaps because you wonder if you did something to contribute to this result.

It is natural to feel angry, but remember that although you may seek to blame other people, your judgement of situations will have been altered by the intensity of your feelings after a loss.

Sadness and depression

Many people go through periods of weeping and feeling extremely low after a death. The same happens after the loss of a job. Not everyone automatically cries, but if you don't, this does not mean that your feelings are any less intense. Most people report having 'bad days and good days'. They find they can hardly get up to face one day, but the next they find they can cope with some simple tasks. Feeling low after a death or a job loss can be very long lasting. If you feel trapped in a downward spiral of depression that goes on for months, seek help from your GP.

Longing and yearning

The desire to turn the clock back and change the last words you exchanged with a partner, to see them again or to tell a partner something important, are all recognised as part of the grieving process. Some people visit the grave to 'talk' to the dead person, or believe they see them again.

Where the loss of a job is concerned, you may want to revisit the workplace or to see former colleagues.

If you are on the firing end and were instrumental in terminating someone's employment, only to regret it, you might end up visiting the site of the employee, ie his or her house. I'm not recommending this as a course of action, but let me tell you about a real example in which someone's employment was terminated in a heated moment after a falling-out with their boss.

The person was a top class candidate in a senior role. It was a brilliant job and company. Each side indicated some willingness to fix things up but both (tough cookies) found it difficult to pluck up the nerve to make the next move. Almost a year after the relationship ended, the person who'd lost their job had the feeling that the former employer would be in their house, although they never before had been there. So, this person had their house painted.

One Sunday morning a couple of weeks later, the person opened the front door on the way to the gym and outside the garden there stood the former employer! He wasn't alone and, embarrassed at being found out, fled. Actually, his former employee would have liked to speak to him and, had he been alone, would simply have invited him in.

Sounds mad, doesn't it? Well, it is a bit unusual, but it's not mad. In this particular case, the *specific* circumstances that had taken place beforehand made it perfectly plausible. He is not a stalker (and I am not recommending that any reader becomes one!).

My point is that there is not always a textbook solution to every situation; the 'human condition' is very important.

Anyway, this desire to revisit is natural. It can be helped by talking to someone you trust. Tell them what you would have said if you had had the chance.

Managing bereavement

Recovering from bereavement is not something on which you can expect to have a fixed timeframe. There is no law that says that you should be over a human bereavement one year or ten years after it happens.

But most people gradually find that they reach an equilibrium, when the raw pain of the event has passed. Over months and years you may find that life begins to be more manageable - although nothing will take away the reality of the loss. You are likely to complete the bereavement process that follows a workplace loss more quickly than a death. That's because you can replace a job, you can't replace a human being who has died.

Things that may help you to cope

Tell the story of what happened to people you trust. Telling and retelling your story can help you make sense of what has happened. You may prefer not to discuss the matter; that's fine too, though it may take a little longer to put the event behind you.

Keep a journal of your experiences. This is an established technique to help with the expression of grief. If you enjoy painting or making music, this can also prove a creative outlet.

Take your time in sorting out clothes and other personal possessions of the dead person. Keep in mind that if you take instant decisions on this, you may come to regret it.

If you are experiencing bereavement after the loss of a job, then deal with the paperwork, your ID card, old payslips. Stick them in a box in the attic; it will not help you regularly to come across reminders of a lost job all over the house.

Share any concerns about finances or residential problems. Don't be afraid to ask for help from those who can support you and/or your bank and mortgage lender.

In the case of a death, once the funeral and early weeks are past, consider marking the death in some way. You could give some money to a favourite charity, plant a tree or buy a picture as a memorial of the person you loved. This can be comforting, as well as a 'rite of passage' after a bereavement. A 'rite of passage' after the loss of a job could be to meet up socially with former colleagues to catch up on what you are all doing now.

You can't seem to stop dwelling on a negative work-related matter

Sometimes a bad work experience plays itself over and over in your mind like a scratched record. How can you stop this obsessive thinking?

There is a very simple solution to this dilemma. When the negative sound track starts up in your mind, tell yourself STOP.

That's right. Stop.

Say it out loud to yourself if it helps.

It works.

You can also use this technique to help in other ways, such as improving your time management. If you find that you dither and it takes you ages to complete a task that should take a much shorter length of time, it is likely that you are easily distracted. Use the *Stop!* technique to help you focus on the task in hand.

Keep an eye on body language

Travelling on business? Open your eyes. Observe every action. And learn. Normal everyday Irish gestures are very much different to those used abroad. There are a lot of gestures that could be interpreted incorrectly. Body language has always been very important in relation to dealing with people in the workplace. Travel around the world and you may find it is something that requires a lot of skill to master.

A business trip to India highlighted an often-overlooked clue to better understanding a culturally diverse workplace. Body language.

The exhibition hall at Bangelore's Raj Hotel buzzed as a group of Irish-based technology companies courted candidates interested in moving in Ireland. My role was to host information seminars on working and living in Ireland. The seminar room was packed to capacity, the audience lively and keen to interact.

Why, then, were all three hundred people vigorously shaking their heads from side to side - which in Ireland would equate to a very loud non-verbal "NO". I had to ask. Their sense of humour tickled, the audience was quick to explain. In India this head movement signifies an expression of extreme interest, the equivalent of an Irish audience nodding their heads.

Some nationalities are more reserved than others, so don't just wait for what they say, watch the body language.

Expect the Unexpected

Aware that the people of India are somewhat reserved, I wasn't surprised to find that they don't applaud by clapping. What was unexpected was the way, at what I thought was the end of the seminar, the entire group surrounded me to ask questions so that I couldn't turn without bumping into someone. I was quite literally mobbed.

Keep an eye on body language

A little too close to comfort even for most Europeans who have an 'intimate distance' of 20-30 cms (8-12inches). You might however expect the laid-back Australians to get close; not so, like the Americans, Australians are comfortable at a distance of 46 - 122 cms (18-49nches) while a comfortable intimate distance for a Japanese person is around 25 cms (10-11 inches).

Next time you are in a group with mixed nationalities, notice how those present move as they talk to each other. Those who stand still as they converse are comfortable with the distance between them. Those who move as they speak are not - the person requiring a greater distance will move back from the other, while the one requiring less distance moves closer - and so it continues.

Even something as simple as a handshake assumes different meanings in different cultures. Generally, people shake hands the first time they meet, in some Asian cultures older women bow with their hands in front of their face as though in prayer and in yet other cultures the hand shaking never stops. I am reminded of one company where a large contingent of German nationals moved to Ireland for a year and shook hands with each of their Irish colleagues as they greeted them every single day. Long before the end of their stay the accompanying humourous comments had become part of the ritual.

Careful Interpretation

Interpreting a kiss is another minefield. Exchanged only in private and between married couples in some parts of the world, the French *baiser* - that's the air-kiss, not French kissing! - is universally popular among Europeans. Best advice? Don't kiss until you have first been kissed.

Before the current boom, chances are we've all had to thumb a lift at some point. Easy enough in Ireland, the UK and Australia. In Greece, however, the same thumbs-up means 'get stuffed'. And what if you don't speak Greek, never mind you could use the 'OK' or ring gesture to signal your understanding. Maybe. In France, this gesture literally means 'nothing', in Japan it can refer to money and in American 'OK'. Careful about using this gesture to men in some European countries, however, you may be implying that they are gay.

All this hassle before you've uttered a word. At least you'll be safe raising your two fingers in victory anywhere in the world - with your palm facing *outwards* of course.

With the current emphasis on cultural diversity, how can you avoid putting your foot in it?

You are working with colleagues of several different nationalities and cultures. Everyone's approach is different and you feel you're walking on eggshells

When you're working in a culturally diverse workforce, it is a smart move to increase your awareness of cultural differences.

You may never have had much reason actually to reflect on cultural differences. It is more usual simply to stereotype the differences, perhaps based on the *explicit culture* that you have observed.

Explicit culture includes food, language, buildings, houses, monuments, agriculture, shrines, markets, fashions and art. These things symbolise a deeper level of culture. These symbols are also the starting point of prejudices. For instance, consider what you think about Germans when on holiday they occupy all the spaces by the pool from dawn (or so it seems).

This does not really tell us a great deal about German culture in terms of its values, but it is pretty annoying and can lead us to jump to conclusions about the kind of people Germans really are.

You really don't need this kind of cultural misperception or misunderstanding to jeopardise your success at work.

That's why it is important to explore the **next layer of culture: norms and value**s.

Norms are the shared sense that a group has of what is "right" and "wrong". Norms develop formally (eg laws) and informally (eg in the way society controls itself).

Values determine the definition of "good and bad" and accordingly are closely related to the ideals shared by a group.

Norms give us a sense of how we **should** behave, **values** give us a sense of how we **aspire** to behave.

An entire industry sector is devoted to cultural diversity. The leading research considers how cultures differ depending on three factors:

1.   Our relationships with other people: the answers to the following questions vary hugely from culture to culture and tell you a great deal about that culture

- Which matters most - rules or relationships?
- Which is more important - the group or the individual?
- What is considered an acceptable degree of involvement in relationships – keeping work and private life totally separate, or getting to know your colleagues and clients on a personal and family level?
- What do we consider to be a 'normal' expression of feelings? Businesslike handshakes among colleagues who see each other regularly (common in German workplace) or air-kissing men and women alike (France)?
- How do we accord status? Do we ask *what* you studied (ie what you have achieved) or *where* you studied (how prestigious was the establishment)

2.   Issues relating to time
Our cultural perception of time manifests itself in two ways. The first is how we regard the **structure of time.**

People from cultures that view time as a series of passing events tend to do one thing at a time, and prefer planning and keeping to plans once they have been made. Time commitments are taken very seriously and staying on schedule is a must.

Other cultures view the past, present and future as being interrelated. They usually do several things at once. Time commitments are desirable but are not absolute and plans are changed easily.

The second way in which time shapes cultures is the **relative importance placed on the past, present and future.**

Northern Ireland is an example of where the past and its traditions are significant. This doesn't mean people in that culture don't look to the future, simply that the past is important to them.

In a culture predominantly oriented towards the present (eg America), day-to-day experiences tend to direct people's lives. The result of the Presidential election is evidence of that.

In a future-oriented culture, most human activities are directed toward future prospects. In this case, the past is not considered to be vitally significant to the future.

3.   The meaning people assign to their environment

This is best illustrated by examples. The chairman of Sony, Mr Motita, explained how he came to conceive of the Walkman. He loves classical music and wanted to have a way of listening to it on his way to work without bothering any fellow commuters. The Walkman was a way of not imposing on the outside world, but of being in harmony with it. Contrast that to the way most westerners think about using the device. "I can listen to music without being disturbed by other people."

Another example is the use of facemasks over the nose and mouth. Ask someone in Tokyo why they wear it and you'll be told that when people have colds or a virus they wear masks to avoid polluting or infecting *other* people. In Dublin bikers wear masks to avoid being polluted *by* the environment.

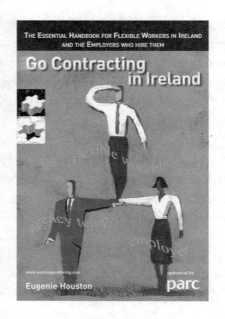

www.smartmovesatwork.com

You didn't ask for one, but apparently you're getting a new employer!

You work in the IT department in a financial services firm. One of the best names in the country. Though you're an adventurous type, the terms, conditions and prospects are so good that you think you will stay in this employment for years, maybe even until you retire. Then you are informed that the entire function is to be outsourced and you will effectively have a new employer. What rights do you have in a transfer situation?

The law provides that the rights and obligations of the original employer (arising from an employment contract existing at the date of a transfer) transfer to the new employer. This includes a transfer of your length of service.

Furthermore, the new employer must continue to observe the terms and conditions agreed in any collective agreement on the same terms that applied to the old employer until the collective agreement expires or is replaced.

Both the original and new employers are obliged to inform their respective employees' representatives of the date of the transfer, the reasons for the transfer and the legal, social and economic implications of the transfer. This must be done, where reasonably practicable, not later than 30 days before the transfer date, and in any event in good time before the transfer is carried out (or in the case of the new employer, in good time before the employees are directly affected by the transfer regarding conditions of employment).

Details of any measures envisaged in relation to the employees must be discussed with the employees' representatives "with a view to reaching an agreement". Where there are no representatives, the employers must arrange for the employees to choose representatives for this purpose.

What if an employee is dismissed following a transfer?

An employee may not be dismissed because of a transfer. Dismissals for "economic, technical or organisational reasons entailing changes in the workforce" are, however, allowed.

If an employee's contract of employment is terminated because a transfer involves a substantial change in working conditions to the detriment of the employee, the employer concerned is regarded as having been responsible for the termination.

Can your temporary employer stop you from taking a permanent job elsewhere in the organisation?

You have been working for a bank on a temporary basis, and have twice asked your manager about his plans for you. He never responded. Now you have been offered full-time work in another department but your manager refuses to let you go. What is the best way to gain that position without upsetting your current boss?

Communication is the key. You are right to ask for feedback about the organisation's plans for you. Even if they don't know at the moment it would be helpful if they told you that.

There's no point try to second-guess why your manger didn't come back to you and now doesn't want to let you go. Probably because you are so valuable in your current role!

First, decide what you want. Is it clarification of your opportunities? Knowing what specific plans they have for you, if any? Getting the job in the other department?

Be positive. Ask for a meeting, telling your manager in advance what specifically you need to discuss. In preparation for your meeting, review the notes on effectively selling earlier in **Smart Moves at Work**. Approach the meeting constructively. "I have enjoyed working here because.......as I am ambitious........clarifying what we both want helps us to move ahead constructively".

If your aim is to get the job in the other department, ask "what would I need to do/ or what would need to happen in order for me to get that job? Then use whatever information emerges as the basis of your next step. Ask the current manager if he can help you.

What is the difference between an interim manager and a consultant?

A reader to the Daily Telegraph wrote: What do you call someone who knows 100 ways to make love and nobody to do it with? - A consultant!

Interim management is the temporary appointment of a senior independent executive or manager by an organisation for a defined period, either to undertake a change programme or project, or to take on a specified role. An interim management placement is a flexible resource used for a limited time and often arranged at short notice.

Interim management is also known as head-renting or executive leasing. The interim manager may also be called an executive temp, company doctor, temporary executive, portfolio manager or leased manager.

Although interim management is widely used across all sectors it occupies only a relatively small though growing segment of the total professional services to organisations. Initially interim managers were used in manufacturing industries but they are now to be found in all sectors including local authorities.

A **consultant makes recommendations** to an organisation's management team whereas an **interim manager delivers** outcomes from planning through to implementation, review and handover.

An interim manager **reports** directly to the **employing organisation's senior management** unlike a management consultant who still **reports to his or her consultancy**. Interim managers may have line management responsibility. Interim managers are practical hands-on managers, with well-developed interpersonal skills, who must get results.

254

How much will an interim manager cost?

Initially, it may appear that using interim managers is an expensive option. The range of fees quoted per day in various sources is very wide, though a useful guide is 1.2% - 1.4% of the annual salary that would be offered.

To work out a daily rate, divide the gross by 232 not 365. (You exclude 104 weekend days, 20 days' annual leave and 9 public holidays).

It is hard to directly compare the daily fees of an interim manager with the equivalent daily cost of a full time employee. Organisations do not have to pay the following costs associated with hiring permanent employees:

- Recruitment fees
- Pension
- Company car, private health insurance etc
- Holiday pay
- Sick pay
- Severance pay
- Training and development opportunities.

Taking all additional costs into account, an interim manager often costs no more than a new permanent employee. Furthermore, as a high calibre executive, the interim manager represents good value for money and is a cost-effective solution to resource problems.

You want a permanent contract

You have been employed on a series of 13 fixed-term contracts for more than nine years, doing work that is directly comparable to that of permanent colleagues. Can you force your employer to make you a permanent member of staff?

In July 2003, the Protection of Employees (Fixed-Term Work) Act was passed into law. Prior to that, contractors had no employment protection. This law does not apply to agency temps.

The Act limits the use of successive fixed-term contracts. Now a fixed-term employee may be renewed on only one further occasion (without any restrictions on the duration at that time) after the fixed-term employee has completed at least 3 years of continuous employment. So a fixed-term worker could in his or her fourth year of employment receive one final – and perhaps very long – fixed-term contract.

This makes Ireland the most flexible EU state in this regard. In the UK for instance, fixed-term contracts can be renewed for just four successive years. The legislation applies from July 2003.

The Act brought into law a number of other protections for fixed-term workers.

This and many other matters are dealt with in detail in my books *Go Contracting in Ireland* and *Go Contracting in the UK.* See **www.smartmovesatwork.com** for more details

Your 4-month temp-to-perm contract was terminated after a week as the person decided to stay. Can they just change their minds?

You have had a 4-month temp-to-perm contract terminated after just a week because the person you were replacing decided to stay. You were paid for the days worked plus one month in lieu. Is there any other remedy you can seek as you turned down other jobs for this?

Your best approach is probably to take the money and run. You have in effect been paid in part for the remainder of the three-month period.

Whether or not you have an actual contract is important. If you do have a 3-month fixed term contract with no notice clause, then you can enforce it and look for the full difference of money due. I doubt that this is what your contract says but do check.

If you were placed by an agency and are on the agency's payroll (highly probable) then your employment relationship is with the agency; check their terms and conditions. I'm afraid you will find these favour the agency, not you, in this instance.

What should you look for in a good interim manager?

An interim manager is selling his or her expertise. This expertise will be highlighted by responsibilities held, outcomes achieved, and range of roles previously undertaken, maybe including multi-country exposure. Look for expertise in a significant area of activity eg finance, Human Resources, IT, sales, marketing, general management.

Do you need someone with a background at board level or who has been directly answerable to the board?

Is the candidate more than qualified for the role they are taking on, therefore needing no training?

Will the interim be able to take on high-level responsibility at short notice and then be effective immediately?

Is he or she flexible enough to extend an initial contract as long as necessary to complete the project?

Highly developed interpersonal skills and a strong, independent and self-sufficient personality are always needed together with the ability to lead, organise and motivate.

Is the person focused on completing the job in hand and happy to be measured on results?

A good interim will need to be enthusiastic for his or her role and able to adapt into different organisation cultures.

Will this person be able to move on when the job is finished? This is important. Although some interims take assignments while they actively seek permanent roles, the best interims are people who relish being self-employed and will be happy to leave the assignment, as a job well done, on completion.

Many people seeking work as interim managers for the first time are looking for new challenges or a better work-life balance. They are generally aged over 35 with at least 10 years' experience at senior level.

What roles are open to interim managers?

Circumstances that often lead to the use of interim managers include:

- Restructuring of organisations which can reduce readily available in-house expertise competently to oversee change activities
- Temporarily vacant senior positions
- The need for organisations to undertake strategic change.

The role will be at a senior level and it may be either a stopgap position to provide continuity, strategic placement to develop the business or a project placement to achieve a defined aim.

Stopgap roles include:
- A short-term replacement for a senior executive who is either absent from work or temporarily working elsewhere in the organisation
- A temporary appointment, following the departure of a senior executive, until the permanent post is filled

Strategic placements include:
- Leading a major change programme such as a reorganisation or restructuring
- Handling a merger, flotation, acquisition or disposal
- Resolving a crisis

Project placements include:
- Running a short term or one-off project such as a major IT development or a new product launch that requires expertise not available in house
- Establishing and defining a new role that will subsequently be filled permanently.

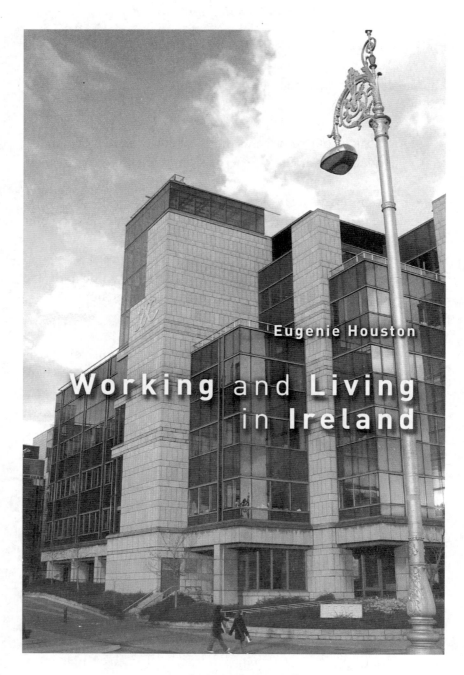

Eugenie Houston

Working and Living in Ireland

www.smartmovesatwork.com

Can you leave before you've even started?

You have recently signed a contract of employment, but have subsequently been offered a much better position with another employer. What are the legal consequences of cancelling the contract previously signed?

The consequences depend on a number of issues, including whether your contract contained a specific start date, the seniority of the post involved and whether the new job is with a competitor. Following are the main factors you will need to consider.

Start date

If the contract of employment contains a specific start date then failing to attend work on that date will constitute a breach of contract (unless you are absent for any authorised reason, eg sickness).

If the contract does not contain a different start date, eg it is just "to be agreed", arguably the contract is not sufficiently certain to be relied on by the employer.

An agreement to agree in the future is not legally binding and, therefore, if the contract cannot stand as it is written without any further terms being agreed to, it will not necessarily be enforceable.

Breach of contract

If the contract does contain a definite start date and you are not going to attend work and have no legitimate reason for your absence, consequences for breach of contract will need to be considered.

The courts are very reluctant to compel an employee to work for an employer and, accordingly, it is extremely unlikely that the employer could obtain specific performance of the contract requiring you to work.

However, as with any breach of contract claim the wronged party is entitled to damages which put him or her in a position in which he or she could have been had the contract been performed, *provided* the losses flow naturally from the breach.

This normally means the cost of a temporary replacement but there could be other losses if, for example, you are a senior manager or director who is bringing clients with you and other senior candidates who could have also done so have now been rejected.

Notice of termination

There is nothing to prevent the employee giving notice under the terms of the contract. This notice will run from the start date not beforehand. If, prior to the start of the contract, you write to the employer indicating that you are giving notice or will give notice on the first day of your employment, practically speaking it is unlikely that most employers will want an employee to start working for them when they are only going to be there for the notice period.

Restrictive covenants

The situation may well be more complicated if the contract contains valid restrictive covenants, especially if one is a non-compete clause and the offer of alternative employment is from a competitor.

In this scenario, the first employer may well wish to prevent the employment of the employee by the second employer. Accordingly, the first employer might write to the second employer warning them that by employing you they will be inducing a breach of contract, which is a cause of action in the civil courts.

Exiting your job

It is possible to obtain an injunction to prevent such an act being committed. Whether this is a realistic concern obviously depends upon the circumstances of your specific case and the enforceability of any restrictive covenants.

Assuming that the contract does contain a definite start date, that you are not a particularly senior or vital member of staff for the new employer, the contract contains no restrictive covenants and that the offer is not from a competitor, the practical answer to the question is that while there are legal consequences, the employer is not likely to take action.

In this case, the most practical way of dealing with the problem is writing to the first employer and explaining that you will be giving notice on the first day of the employment and asking whether or not, in the circumstances, the employer actually wishes you to commence employment with them.

It is possible to terminate a contract by mutual agreement. How successful this strategy will be will obviously depend on how much the employer needs your skills.

What is the difference between resignation, dismissal and redundancy?

You are on the verge of quitting your job after 10 years. You wonder if you would be better off being made redundant, resigning or being dismissed. In all of these eventualities, are you entitled to any severance pay?

I've lost count now of the number of times I have been asked this question. Put this way, your question gives the impression that you are quitting voluntarily. Of course, you may feel you are being forced to leave, in which case it may be a constructive dismissal. Or your job may cease to exist, in which case redundancy would apply.

No matter how long you've spent in your job, the fact that your employer previously may have made redundancies and/ or paid off people just to get rid of them, you will not have an automatic entitlement to a 'settlement' simply because you now want to leave. I make this point strongly, because it addresses a common misperception.

Let's assume for now that you want to leave. If this is the case, then you should resign, giving the appropriate amount of notice. With 10 years' service, you will be statutorily required to give and receive 6 weeks notice. Do check to see whether your contract stipulates a longer notice period; if it does, the longer period will apply.

It will then be up to your employer to decide whether you have to work out your notice period. A number of possibilities may then occur.

The first is that your employer requires you to work your notice, so you will work and be paid up to the last day of employment. It is unlikely that any other payment will be owing to you, except for any outstanding pay and/or expenses due to you.

The second is that your employer requires you to remain employed but does not want you in the office. You will be asked to remain at home on "garden leave" but should still receive full pay until your last day of employment. This is not at all unusual in senior roles. You might equally be required to sit out garden leave if you leave a competitive environment, such as a recruitment agency.

The third is that your employer will agree to release you from your notice period, in which case you will be free to leave, but will receive no further pay.

The fourth is that your employer could ask you to leave immediately and pay you in lieu of your notice period. Pay in lieu of notice in this way is generally exempt from the deduction of income tax (because it is not paid while you are in employment), but check your own situation.

Finally, you could leave giving less than your contractual notice. Technically you will be in breach of contract and your employer may decide to take further action against you to claim back any losses suffered as a result of your premature departure.

In practice, few employers are keen to embark on such litigation. However, every case will be different and it will depend on the terms of each individual contract. For example some contracts contain post employment restrictions and employers are likely to be very keen to ensure that these restrictions are honoured, especially where the employee has breached the notice provisions in the contract. I don't recommend leaving with insufficient notice.

If your **resignation is not voluntary**, ie you consider yourself to have been constructively dismissed, then you are entitled to your notice payments, and, if you succeed in proving your case at a Tribunal, (provided you have at least one year's service with your employer) compensation for unfair dismissal.

If you are dismissed with notice (fairly and following fair procedure), you will receive notice payment in lieu of notice.

If you are made redundant, you will receive your contractual notice and a statutory redundancy payment (provided you have at least two years service at the date of your redundancy). Your employer may operate a redundancy scheme that is more favourable than the statutory scheme.

Whether you are dismissed or made redundant is a matter for your employer at the end of the day and you are unlikely to be able to influence their decision one way or the other.

But to come back to your question, you are not being asked to leave, but appear to have decided to leave. If you are in any doubt about who is was that indicated a desire for you to leave (you or the employer?), then think about it and act on your concerns **before** you leave.

Can you get redundancy instead of resigning?

You are currently awaiting an offer letter with terms of employment from a new employer. After being with your current employer for seven years, you'd like to be able to negotiate a redundancy package rather then resign without any compensation? Would this jeopardise your new job when accepted?

A very similar question to the previous one. The short answer to your question is that you can't claim redundancy simply on the basis of seven years' service. The legal definition of redundancy covers three situations:

1) Where the employer closes down the business altogether
2) Where the employer closes down the employee's workplace, and
3) Where the job disappears - either because there is less work or because fewer employees are required to do it.

If your situation corresponds to one of the above you may be able to claim a redundancy payment.

Alternatively, if your current employer is offering voluntary redundancy packages then you would be advised to volunteer for redundancy before you resign.

If you are not entitled to (or offered) a redundancy package, you have no leverage to request "compensation" from your current employer. You are the party that wishes to leave the employment relationship, not your employer and you have no entitlement to any additional compensation. The reality is that you've already been compensated for the work you've done – you have received your salary to date.

You will, however, be entitled to your notice pay. When you resign, your employer may pay you a sum in lieu of your notice pay (where it has a contractual right to do so) or it may require you to work out your notice period.

If you are subject to a genuine redundancy situation (as defined above) or you accept a voluntary redundancy package from your current employer, there will be no adverse legal effect on your new job.

If you try to engineer a redundancy situation where none exists, you are likely to damage your chances of a great reference from your employer.

How long before they can legally rehire?

If you are made redundant, after what time period can your employer recruit someone else into the same role? Can you then claim unfair dismissal?

The simple answer is that there is no minimum or maximum time period during which your employer cannot hire somebody to carry out a role similar to yours, but in doing so they raise the question of whether or not your position was genuinely redundant.

If your position was not genuinely redundant, you may be entitled to bring a claim for unfair dismissal. If you did bring a claim in the tribunal, your employer would be required to prove that there was a genuine redundancy situation and that it dismissed you in a procedurally fair manner.

The definition of redundancy falls into three categories: closure of an entire business; closure of your particular place of work or a reduced or no need for employees to carry out the particular kind of work which you carry out.

It is usually fairly clear if either of the first two categories genuinely apply. The third is more difficult but the employer will need to show that it needs fewer or no employees to carry out work of a particular kind. This may be due to a drop-off in orders or clients and if these subsequently pick up the employer may need to re-hire. However, the shorter the period of time after your dismissal in which somebody is hired to carry out your role, the greater the suspicion that your role was not genuinely redundant in the first place.

The other point that you should bear in mind is that you are normally required to bring a claim for unfair dismissal within six months beginning with the date of your dismissal. This time limit is interpreted strictly, but you may be able to have a claim considered outside the normal time period in exceptional circumstances where it was not reasonably practicable for you to present your claim within the time period.

If you do take a claim in the Employment Appeals Tribunal and win, the Tribunal will take into account any compensation you have received already, ie your redundancy package.

Please keep in mind the central tenet of this book: it is important to know your rights and receive them. It is also important that where your rights are infringed that you consider what it best for you. Consider the potential legal costs and the amount of time you may spend (and waste) worrying about someone else getting your job down the line.

Consider if this time would not be better spent getting a new job and getting on with your life. Of course, if you are made redundant, ensure you receive your statutory entitlements. These days, many companies offer generous enhanced packages to ease the pain.

You want to leave during your probationary period

After a period of redundancy you recently joined a company paying you considerably less than you were hoping for. Two weeks after starting work you have been offered a much more desirable position elsewhere. Despite being in a three-month probationary period you are still expected to give one month's notice. Is it reasonable that you should have to work the month?

The short answer is that you do have to work out the agreed notice, unless you can come to an alternative agreement with your employer.

When you entered into a contract of employment with your current employer, you accepted a three-month probationary period during which the notice required by either side would be one month. Accordingly, in order to terminate your contract of employment without giving rise to a breach of contract, you must give your employer notice as prescribed in the contract. In the event that you terminate your contract of employment without providing your employer with the requisite period of notice, your employer may seek some form of remedy for the breach of contract. The likelihood of your employer pursuing such action will depend on the effect your departure will have on their business. The possible claims your employer may have against you in such circumstances are as follows:

The first is a claim for damages for breach of contract. Damages can only be sought if your employer has suffered loss as a result of your failure to give notice as provided in your contract. If your employer cannot prove any loss, it would be pointless for them to seek damages.

The second possibility is for your employer to seek an injunction against you, your new employer or possibly both. However, in order to do so, they would need to show a serious risk of loss to their business. Therefore, if there is no serious risk of loss to your employer's business, then granting of an injunction would be unlikely.

The third potential claim would be for your current employer to bring an action for inducing breach of contract against your new employer. However, your current employer would need to show that your new employer knew of the existing contract and, more importantly, the clause stipulating the notice period and, furthermore, that they knowingly induced a breach of that particular clause. Again, much would depend on the specific circumstances of the case.

If you decide to give your employer notice of the termination of your employment, you will be expected to work during the course of that month unless there is an express "garden leave" clause in the contract, giving your employer the legal right to require that you stay at home during the notice period.

You think you're being set up

You have worked for well-known company the last 5 years and your firm is currently undergoing drastic cuts. Either you will be fired or officially reprimanded over a trivial matter, which before the new regime came in, was established practice. You believe your managers are doing this to 'tie' you to the firm in some way. If you accept the official warning will this go on your file and will it affect your future prospects? You are considering resigning instead of taking this warning if it will stop you moving to another bank. If they are considering firing you, how do you go about ensuring you get a decent severance or is it out of your hands?

Let me clarify my understanding of your position. You are currently subject to disciplinary proceedings, which may result in your dismissal or a warning. You are considering resigning from your job before these proceedings are decided because you are concerned that if you get a warning it will affect your ability to secure alternative employment.

Your employer is under an obligation to provide a fair and honest reference about you on request. However, this obligation does not prevent your employer from stating that you are currently subject to disciplinary proceedings or you have received a disciplinary warning, if those statements are true.

If your employer wishes to be unhelpful by not providing you with a positive reference it may do so as long as what they do say about you is truthful. You will have no recourse against your current employer for making such statements unless those statement are misleading or untrue.

I would advise that at present you stay and fight the disciplinary proceedings. When you know the outcome you will be better placed to decide how to proceed. If you leave now, you will forfeit your rights to a redundancy payment and your employers will be entitled to say that you resigned from the company during disciplinary proceedings, which could look bad to potential employers.

Your bargaining position for negotiating a severance package will depend on the terms of your employment contract and, if you are dismissed, it will also depend on the circumstances of your dismissal which may give rise to a statutory claim for unfair dismissal. You should contact an employment lawyer to discuss these issues in more detail.

Is gardening leave enforceable?

You have just accepted a new job offer, but have a six-month garden leave clause in your existing contract. Is there any way you can escape from the full six months?

A "garden leave" clause is a clause that allows an employer to ask an employee to work out his notice from home while continuing to be paid in the normal way. The idea is that this will be enough time for you to empty your mind of all of the company's secret information and to lose contact with important business contacts, with which you may have had regular contact. Gardening leave basically takes you out of the market for that time period.

It is often used where an employee has given notice that he wishes to join a competitor and allows the employer to keep him out of the marketplace for the notice period so as to protect the employer's trade secrets and business connections.

Such a clause is perfectly valid, though you will not find one in most ordinary employment contracts. Provided your employer has not breached the contract and has made it clear they wish to hold you to it, the clause may be enforceable.

If you choose to ignore it, then you could expect your employer to seek one of two remedies:

An injunction against you and your new employer, preventing you from working for the new employer for the garden leave period.

Damages against both you and your new employer. Damages would be awarded if the previous employer could show loss (for example, through misuse of confidential information).

However, you should be aware that injunctions are not granted automatically. Your previous employer will only be able to obtain an injunction to hold you to the garden leave where they can show that there is risk of serious harm to their business if you are allowed to join a competitor straight away. An example of such serious harm would be where you are in a position to pass on trade secrets or to take unfair advantage of previous client connections and contacts.

Can you still get redundancy?

You have just been made redundant after two and a half years. As part of the consultation process you expressed interest in working for the company's operation in The Netherlands while commuting back on the weekends. As it turns out the offer made is a local package, which represents a 40% pay cut. Can you turn down this offer and still be entitled to a redundancy package?

Based on the scenario outlined, you should not lose your entitlement to a redundancy payment.

You will only lose your right to a redundancy payment if you unreasonably refuse an offer of suitable alternative employment. The fact that the position would require you to accept a 40 per cent reduction in pay would point to the unsuitability of the offer.

Whether your refusal is reasonable or unreasonable depends entirely on factors personal to you. However, any significant reduction in salary will almost certainly make it reasonable for you to refuse the offer, even if those are the prevailing local market conditions in that country.

On this basis, if you were to reject the offer, the company would have to honour any redundancy payment.

An alternative to rejecting the offer at this stage would be to accept the offer on a trial basis. As the terms and conditions are not identical to your previous terms and conditions, you would be entitled to a statutory trial period of at least 4 weeks. If, during the course of this trial period, you felt that the position was not appropriate for you, you will remain entitled to receive a redundancy payment.

Is this reorganisation really redundancy?

Your company is reorganising and the job you have been doing for 15 years is being split between three posts. Your employer says that you are not in a redundancy situation because there are no fewer jobs in the new set up. It says you must compete internally for any job you are interested in. What can you do?

As your employer still needs employees to carry out work of the kind that you currently do (and because there are no fewer jobs in the new structure and the workload itself has not reduced), the reason for the disappearance of your job is likely to be reorganisation rather than redundancy.

Nevertheless, it would still be wise for your employer to try and find reasonable alternative employment for you. If you were to complain to an employment tribunal that the disappearance of your job meant that you were unfairly dismissed, your employer would need to show:

- That the dismissal was for another potentially fair reason
- That he acted reasonably in dismissing you. An offer of reasonable alternative employment would help him to do so

Your employer is entitled to insist you enter into a competitive (internal) recruitment process for any jobs you are interested in, although again a tribunal would consider whether this was reasonable in all the circumstances. It may be that your employer sees this as being the fairest way of employees obtaining jobs they would be happy with and, as the number of employees your employer needs overall is the same, it seems likely that you will be offered a job once you have been through this stage.

Alternatively, it may be company policy that new posts should be advertised or that the new jobs have an important new dimension and as a result your employer feels it necessary for you to go through the recruitment process.

Although an offer of employment involving a demotion or a reduction in pay or status can be a reasonable one (depending on *all* the circumstances), a tribunal would probably consider it unreasonable to expect you to go through the recruitment process to obtain such an offer.

Your employer sacked you without notice when you resigned

When you resigned from your previous job, the company said they were going to dismiss you anyway that day because they had found out you had deleted personal emails from your PC. They refused your resignation and consequently paid you no notice or holiday due. Are they allowed to do that?

You can be dismissed for gross misconduct even after you have resigned, but the deletion of personal e-mails would certainly not appear to represent gross misconduct.

To deprive you of your notice entitlement, it would be necessary for you to have committed a breach of your employment contract justifying summary termination. It would also be necessary for the employer to carry out a **fair procedure** culminating in the dismissal.

It would be more normal for an employer to have concerns regarding the deletion of professional e-mails or the unauthorised copying of information belonging to the employer.

In any event you would almost certainly be entitled to your accrued holiday entitlement. The only situation where this would potentially not be the case would be if the contract of employment expressly provided that on summary termination no accrued entitlement would be paid.

However, even in this situation there would be a strong argument that an entitlement would exist to at least the statutory minimum holiday entitlement.

What should you consider before accepting redundancy?

You are about to be made redundant as your company is relocating. They have asked you to sign an agreement what will entitle you to a payment on top of your statutory redundancy money. This agreement is very lengthy and exonerates them for everything after you have left. They have also recommended that you get independent legal advice before signing. What should you be wary of if you do decide to sign?

The first point is that your employer cannot force you to sign the settlement agreement. If you are being dismissed by reason of redundancy, provided that you have 104 weeks' service or more, you have a legal right to a statutory redundancy payment.

Your employer is making payment of any money in addition to this statutory redundancy sum conditional on signing the agreement.

Your employer may not be entitled to do this if they have previously agreed to provide an enhanced payment either expressly (for example either in your contract of employment or in any staff handbook) or if there is an implied term of your contract by reason of custom and practice, in which case you would be entitled to the enhanced payment even if you did not sign the agreement.

If you do choose to sign the agreement, it can only waive certain statutory rights and your legal adviser will need to advise you in detail on the effects of the agreement. Put simply, you can't agree to put yourself in a worse position by signing away any protection that the law provides you.

Things to bear in mind when considering the agreement are: how any payment is being taxed; what potential claims you are agreeing to waive; for how much money you are waiving any claims; whether you are providing any indemnities or warranties, particularly with regard to tax. If you are indemnifying the company in respect of tax you should try and include in the settlement agreement the right to challenge any assessments. You should also consider carefully the truth of any statements you are signing.

Finally, if a reference is important to you, it is very common for an agreed reference to be attached as a schedule to the agreement and this is something worth bearing in mind.

What constitutes redundancy following a take-over?

If you should want redundancy following a take-over of your employer by another company, what are the criteria against which you may claim constructive dismissal and therefore redundancy?

In this context redundancy occurs where work of a particular kind disappears or is no longer required by the employer.

Where you are given continuing work, but it is not the same work that you previously did, a tribunal would look to a number of factors to decide whether your original job was redundant.

These would include the duties that you had been performing and for how long, the contract of employment and whether the duties are narrowly or widely defined, and whether any change in duties has any knock-on effect, eg in the number of colleagues supervised. Each case will be a question of fact and degree.

In order to claim redundancy you have to be dismissed. A dismissal occurs where either you receive notice of termination from your employer or you resign in circumstances where you believe that your employer has unilaterally broken your contract (this is commonly known as constructive dismissal).

You could claim constructive dismissal either if your duties are unilaterally changed and your old duties no longer exist (this would be constructive dismissal and redundancy) or where you are given new duties but someone else performs the old duties. That would be just constructive dismissal and the remedy would be to pursue an unfair dismissal complaint.

Before resigning you would have to be confident that any variations in the duties were more than just minor and/or that your employer did not have the right under your contract of employment to vary your duties. Most employers include this in their terms and conditions of employment. If they did have such a right, that may scupper a constructive dismissal complaint.

You should also be aware that even if your previous position is redundant, or your employer has unilaterally changed your duties, you may not be eligible for a redundancy payment if your employer has offered you "suitable alternative employment" and you have "unreasonably refused" it.

What are your rights if made redundant?

About 2 weeks ago, you told your boss you were not satisfied with your reviews, and weren't sure about your future with the company, where you have been for 4 years. He suggested he make you redundant, saying you could get a 3-month tax-free severance package. Later, he said they could only do a 2-month payment. What are your compensation rights?

On the brief facts outlined, if your employment is terminated, you will have the following rights and potential claims against your employer.

Accrued salary: First, you would be entitled to receive any accrued but unpaid salary up to the termination date. If your employer fails to make such a payment to you, you could bring a claim in the Employment Appeals Tribunal to recover this money by way of a claim for unlawful deduction of wages (or in the civil courts for breach of contract).

Accrued holiday entitlements: You are entitled to be paid for any accrued but untaken statutory holiday entitlement. If your employer fails to make such a payment to you, you could bring a claim to recover this money in the Employment Appeals Tribunal. You may also be entitled to be paid for any accrued but untaken additional contractual holiday entitlement. However, this will depend on the terms of your contract of employment.

Notice period: In the absence of your employer having the right to summarily terminate your contract of employment (for example, if you commit any act which amounts to gross misconduct), you will be entitled to either work out your notice period or receive a payment in lieu of notice.

If your employer fails to allow you to work out your notice period or make such a payment to you, you would be entitled to bring a claim against your employer for breach of contract in the employment tribunal or in the civil courts.

The length of your notice period will either be your entitlement to statutory minimum notice, which in your case, on the basis that you have been continuously employed over 2 years but less than 5 years, will be 2 weeks, or your contractual notice entitlement, whichever is longer.

If you are paid in lieu of your notice period, it may be possible for your employer to make this payment to you tax-free.

Claim for unfair dismissal: As your employer has continuously employed you for over one year, you would be eligible to bring a claim of unfair dismissal in an employment tribunal. If successful, you could be awarded compensation by the tribunal.

The amount of compensation that may be awarded is limited to 104 weeks' remuneration and is based on financial loss, which includes any actual or estimated loss of income attributable to the dismissal, the value of any loss or diminution of statutory redundancy and pensions.

If you are found to have been unfairly dismissed but do not suffer any financial loss, you would still be entitled to a basic award of up to four weeks' remuneration. Where loss is suffered, you *don't* receive the compensation and the basic award.

Statutory redundancy payment: As you have been employed continuously by your employer for over two years, if the reason for the termination of your employment falls within the statutory definition of redundancy (which from the brief facts which you have provided does not appear to be the case) you would be entitled to receive a statutory redundancy payment.

However, you will only receive either a statutory redundancy payment or a basic award.

Can you be relocated out of a job like this?

Your employer is relocating. You have been offered relocation but only if you take a 15% pay cut, which you have declined. Your employer is recruiting to fill your post and you are expected to train the newcomer. The training period is May to August, but this may change. You have been offered no additional pay, but will be looked on more favourably when applying for jobs internally. Should your employer not be offering a written commitment, as to timescale and redundancy package? What are your rights if you refuse to help with the training?

I assume for the purposes of your question that you have worked for your company for at least a year, in which case you have the right not to be unfairly dismissed.

After 104 weeks' continuous service, you have the right to a statutory redundancy payment, although your company may make redundancy payments before two years' service, depending on the terms of its redundancy policy.

In answer to your first question, your right not to be *unfairly dismissed* is relevant. Although a redundancy is a potentially fair reason for dismissal (and you should get written clarification that this is the reason for your dismissal) it will only be fair if your employer has warned you about the possibility of the redundancy and consulted with you beforehand, for the purposes of ensuring that you have been identified correctly as being redundant and also in order to identify whether or not there is suitable alternative employment for you within the company.

Such consultation is a two-way process and you are entitled to expect the company to be as open as possible in terms of providing you with information on when any possible redundancy is likely to take effect, as well as the details of any redundancy package to be offered to you.

You can expect your employer to give you written details about your redundancy and the package closer to when it is likely to take effect. I would expect this to be confirmed when you are advised you are at risk of redundancy.

With regard to your second question, you would be very unwise to refuse to provide training as a refusal might well result in your employer starting disciplinary procedures for misconduct on the basis that you have refused to carry out a reasonable instruction. It might also claim that any enhanced redundancy terms only apply where employees have co-operated.

However, the company should not make its search for suitable employment for you conditional on your co-operation in training the new recruit, as it has an obligation to consider suitable positions for you and should be actively discussing this with you.

Once they have given you notice terminating your contract of employment, they cannot extend this without your consent.

Please take time to read about **Our Lady's Hospital for Sick Children** on the following pages.

Any donations you are able to make will be much appreciated and will make a real difference.

Thank you very much – *Eugenie Houston*

Our Lady's Hospital for Sick Children

Our Lady's Hospital for Sick Children welcomes more then 20,000 inpatients and 90,000 outpatients every year. It is one of the world's largest hospitals devoted to the care of children. Any donations you make to **Our Lady's Hospital for Sick Children** will have a profound effect on the care and treatment it can provide to seriously ill children. **Our Lady's** is Ireland's Centre of Excellence for sick children. Activities include:

❖ A national referral centre for children suffering from Cancer, Leukaemia, Cystic Fibrosis, Heart Disease and Spina Bifida

❖ Pioneering organ transplant and heart surgery in children

❖ Research into the major paediatric diseases and ailments

❖ Diseases now labelled "incurable" can be investigated and eliminated

❖ Benefits children throughout the world through publishing and exchanging its medical and research findings.

❖ Appreciates the efforts of all who support its ongoing campaign for seriously ill children.

No brightness shines like that of hope in a child's eyes

please call 1890 507 508

www.cmrf.org

who can work as a contractor? anyone who works

go contracting in the UK

eugenie houston
www.**working**and**living**.com

charterhouse group
international

www.smartmovesatwork.com

Would you like to see your organisation

featured as a sponsor in this book

or another of

Eugenie Houston's books?

If so, please email your details through the

contact page at

www.workingandliving.com

or phone (+353) 045 883 776